Fly/Ride

Europe

1988

Fly/Ride Europe 1988

Ed Perkins

and
the Editors of
Consumer Reports Books

CONSUMERS UNION • MOUNT VERNON • NEW YORK

Special thanks to John Cross, Lucille Matthews, Mary-Minn Peet, and Kelly Pardi of *Consumer Reports Travel Letter*, San Francisco, and to Margaret Heraty and Alex McWhirter, London.

Fly/Ride Europe 1988 is a Consumer Reports Book published by Consumers Union, the nonprofit organization that publishes *Consumer Reports*, the monthly magazine of test reports, product Ratings, and buying guidance. Established in 1936, Consumers Union is chartered under the Not-For-Profit Corporation Law of the State of New York.

The purposes of Consumers Union, as stated in its charter, are to provide consumers with information and counsel on consumer goods and services, to give information on all matters relating to the expenditure of the family income, and to initiate and to cooperate with individual and group efforts seeking to create and maintain decent living standards.

Consumers Union derives its income solely from the sale of *Consumer Reports* and other publications. In addition, expenses of occasional public service efforts may be met, in part, by nonrestrictive, noncommercial contributions, grants, and fees. Consumers Union accepts no advertising or product samples and is not beholden in any way to any commercial interest. Its Ratings and reports are solely for the use of the readers of its publications. Neither the Ratings nor the reports nor any Consumers Union publications, including this book, may be used in advertising or for any commercial purpose. Consumers Union will take all steps open to it to prevent such uses of its material, its name, or the name of *Consumer Reports*.

Contents

Introduction

Despite a weaker dollar, 1987 was a good year for travel to Europe. Almost as many Americans visited Europe last year as in the boom year of 1985, when the strong dollar made Europe one of the great travel bargains in history.

The outlook for 1988 is less rosy. Unless the dollar recovers from the slump it entered in the summer of 1987, Europe will be expensive in 1988. While airfares will probably not change much, costs at your destination will be high—not high enough to deter you from visiting, but high enough to make it worth your while to buy travel arrangements wisely.

By next summer you'll be able to enjoy nonstop flights to Europe from quite a few more U.S. gateway cities than last year. Long-range versions of the new, smaller wide-body A300s and 767s make it feasible for airlines to offer daily flights to Europe from smaller U.S. cities (for example, Charlotte to London) or from the United States to smaller European cities (for example, New York to Manchester). Since most of these smaller U.S. cities are airline hubs, more and more travelers will be able to avoid the time-consuming and delay-prone connections that are frequent at huge airports like JFK and O'Hare. The bad news is that Economy Class seating is getting worse, not better. The airlines still prefer to use advertising hype rather than genuine quality improvements to lure customers. And to date, no airline has seen fit to extend the idea of daytime eastbound flights (which avoid the extreme discomfort of feeling that you've sat up all night in a sardine can) to any routes other than New York to London, with single daily flights on British Airways and Pan Am.

After the final manuscript of the 1988 edition was completed, Highland Express—a low-fare airline mentioned in chapters 3 and 8—suspended operations. At press time the airline was trying to find financing to get it back in the air for the summer season, but it was too early to confirm whether or not Highland Express would fly again. Meanwhile, Virgin Atlantic offers comparable service and fares.

For this edition, we removed British Caledonian from the listings because of an impending acquisition by British Airways. Although this acquisition has had some delays, we expect that the familiar name and stylish lion logo will have disappeared by the summer of 1988. In addition, British Airways plans to reconfigure its 747 fleet: The superior Economy seating in the convertible section between Business Class and Economy may disappear from some planes this year.

Eurailpass and individual-country rail passes will be slightly more expensive this year. Political problems in the Middle East may drive the cost of gasoline up a bit. Thus, the economic balance may shift a bit toward rail travel, compared with driving a rented car, but probably not enough to warrant a change in your preferred mode of travel.

Again this year, the summer is shaping up as uneventful. And again, that's a favorable projection. Although Europe won't be a bargain, it will remain a great value.

PART I

Guide to North Atlantic Airfares

1

Transatlantic Overview

Getting there may well have been "half the fun" in the days of leisurely steamship travel, but in these days of mass-market jet travel, getting there often involves a lot of hassle, especially if you travel during the busiest seasons. So when it comes to transportation, plan defensively! Good planning and research can ease many travel problems.

OBJECTIVES

As the first step in transportation planning, clarify for yourself—and for your travel agent, if you're dealing with one—exactly what you want for your transportation dollars. Of course, it's impossible for anyone else to identify your detailed personal objectives, but chances are that your major concerns will resemble the following list:

1. to minimize travel costs—either absolutely or in relation to the standards of quality you require
2. to minimize your total travel time and the inevitable hassles of travel
3. to maximize the service and comfort you'll experience dur-

ing your transatlantic crossing, within the constraints of the
fares you're willing to pay
4. to minimize avoidable travel risks—those unhappy sur-
prises that cost you time, money, and often both

For most people, setting objectives means accepting some
trade-offs. You can't expect the same option to give both top-quality
service and low prices. You may opt for the absolute rock-bottom
price, regardless of convenience and comfort, or you may prefer
slightly higher-cost options that provide baseline convenience and
comfort. Perhaps you'll go for considerably higher quality, if you
can get it for a good price.

But wherever you stand, don't start to do any planning, un-
dertake any research, or make any other decisions about any aspect
of your trip until you've identified your objectives.

TRANSPORTATION OPTIONS

Since low costs of some kind are probably an important objective
for you, it's a safe bet that you're among the huge majority of
people who will use one of the three most popular approaches to
minimizing airfare:

1. an Economy Class promotional fare on one of the major
   airlines
2. one of the specialized low-fare airlines
3. a charter

Three other approaches to low airfares are available, and you
may well find that one of them offers substantial reductions, below
the lowest of the better-known alternatives:

1. **bulk fares** on either major or low-fare airlines, purchased
   from a tour operator rather than directly from the airline
2. **discounted tickets** on either major or low-fare airlines, obtained through a discounter or a broker of "last-minute"
   travel bargains
3. **unconventional ticket sources**, especially frequent-flier
   coupons

If you are a member of the minority more concerned with comfort and service than with price, you'll use one of the higher-quality options:

1. **Business Class** on a major or low-fare airline
2. **First Class** on a major or low-fare airline
3. a **Business Class** or **First Class charter**

If you're thinking about going into the eastern Mediterranean—or if you have to make several stops along the way—you may find it cheaper to use one of the special **round-the-world excursion fares** than to take the ordinary round-trip.

Finally, if you can't comply with the various restrictions and uncertainties that accompany most low-fare deals—or if you haven't done your homework—you'll end up paying full-fare Economy Class.

Your key planning question, of course, is how to select your best bet in transatlantic transportation. Given the facts, it's relatively easy. Those four basic travel-planning objectives translate directly into the four Cs of evaluating transatlantic transportation: cost, convenience, comfort, and contingencies. For nearly any traveler, the final selection involves a balance of these four factors, weighted and adjusted in accordance with each traveler's individual needs, attitudes, and priorities.

COMPARING COSTS

You should use the cost of an advance-purchase Economy Class excursion on a major airline (see page 27 for a definition of major airline) as the norm against which to measure all others. This type of fare is usually called **APEX** (an acronym for **advance-purchase excursion**) for transatlantic flights. It's the best standard for three reasons:

- It's the most widely used type of ticket for transatlantic vacation travel.
- It's available for virtually all U.S.-to-Europe routes.
- Unless you opt for a high-quality service, it represents the ceiling on what you should pay—the more interesting low-fare options are all cheaper than APEX.

In their sales materials, airlines usually use full-fare Economy Class as the standard of comparison. The reason is obvious: When compared to full-fare Economy, APEX and similarly priced fares can be touted as fabulous bargains. But full-fare Economy is really an artificial standard, since no cost-conscious vacation or business traveler should actually have to use it.

General Price Levels

Here's approximately how these major options will stack up for 1988, with APEX as the standard of comparison pegged at an index of 100 percent.

APEX	100%
Full Fare Economy	150–250%
Business Class	150–350%
First Class	300–600%
Low-Fare Airline	65–85%
Charter/Bulk Fare	60–80%
First Class Charter	90–120%

Specific 1987 price levels for individual routes are shown in chapter 11; 1988 fares were not available at press time but are expected to be in this range. User fees of $13 are added to the price of each round-trip ticket between the United States and Europe.

On some routes, you'll even find minor differences in fare levels among various airlines for the same fare options. But you'll find substantially greater differences in service quality, comfort, and convenience. Most fares will be competitive: Quality factors will usually dictate your final airline and schedule choice once you've established your preferred fare option.

Geographical Variation Within the United States

At one time all U.S.-to-Europe fares were constructed by combining a standard fare from New York to the European city with a domestic add-on from each U.S. city to New York. Although that system still applies to some types of fares, it is no longer universal, especially for the cheapest tickets. New nonstop service between Europe and the Midwest, the South, and the West Coast has given rise to special direct fares that are much lower than those determined by the earlier add-on system. However, an airline that offers connecting service through New York, for example, might construct its fare this way simply because it's the easiest method. Get more than a single fare quote.

In chapter 11, specific fare comparisons are presented for four geographically representative U.S. gateways: New York, Chicago, Texas (Dallas or Houston, depending on specific direct routes), and the West Coast (with fares that in most cases apply to both Los Angeles and San Francisco).

Seasonal Variations

Demand for transatlantic air travel is quite seasonal. The main peak period is in midsummer—mid-June through mid-September. There's a secondary peak over the year-end holiday season. For years airlines and tour operators have used seasonal pricing as a way to fill planes during the rest of the year.

Virtually everything about your European trip will be better if you can travel off-season. Lower airfares are just the beginning. Off-season flights are sometimes less crowded and therefore more comfortable; service is better. Everything else is less crowded too—museums, churches, the great natural wonders. Europe's real cultural programs are in full swing— the ones put on for Europeans rather than tourists. Hotels are much less crowded, especially in the countryside. You'll seldom need reservations. The weather is usually better, and you can save a lot of money in the warmer-climate countries because you won't have to stay in top-price hotels in order to find air-conditioned rooms. If you're planning a trip to Europe for July or August, the first thing you should do is to consider rescheduling it for May, June, September, or October.

At least three distinct pricing levels will be used on most transatlantic routes during 1988. Most people will be traveling in mid-summer, so peak-season fare levels—specifically peak season APEX fares—provide the most realistic bases for comparison. Again, with peak-season APEX as the norm, at an index of 100 percent, the seasons and their associated fare levels will probably vary as follows:

Peak	May–September	100%
Shoulder	Spring, Fall, December 10–24	80–90%
Basic	Rest of year	60–85%

Specific seasonal dates vary by route. In addition, some routes call for a special top-price "peak of peaks" miniseason in midsummer; others include both "low basic" and "high basic" variants. Finally, supply-and-demand balances are fine-tuned on some routes with differential pricing for midweek trips (lower) and weekend trips (higher). Specific dates—which vary among specific routes—are shown in chapter 11.

Restrictions

Obviously, a very large share of the total vacation-travel market is price sensitive: The higher the prices, the fewer the travelers. So the airlines have to offer low fares to the vacation market. On the other hand, airlines don't want all their passengers, especially business travelers, to pay bottom dollar if they can be charged much higher fares.

What has been the airlines' solution? Simple. Airlines have addressed the vacation market by placing various restrictions on vacation-market fares that make them less appealing or useful to business travelers: advance purchase; round-trip purchase requirements; minimum and maximum lengths of stay; and restrictions or prohibitions on stopovers, standby status, and the like. Business travelers generally find that these restrictions make their travel too inconvenient or too uncertain. However, in most cases only the restrictions and the fares are different—all Economy Class passengers, regardless of the type of fares they pay, fly in the same cabins, and they usually receive the same flight amenities.

Restrictions are most stringent on the major airlines—the ones that have the most to lose if business travelers switch to low-fare services. Still, even low-fare airlines and charters have some restrictions, more often than not imposed by governments to "protect" their major airlines from full open-market competition.

Many of the lowest-price options—especially on the major airlines—are **excursion fares**. That term simply means that a round-trip ticket is required. In most cases, an **open-jaw route** is also acceptable. An open-jaw itinerary also requires purchase of two transatlantic flight segments, but with a difference: You can either fly from a U.S. city to one city in Europe and return to the same U.S. city from another city in Europe, or you can fly from one U.S. city to Europe and return from the same European city to a different U.S. city. On an open-jaw route, transportation between the two European or U.S. gateways can be either by surface transportation or by airline, with a separate ticket.

Status Fares

Some types of airfares include special lower-cost provisions for travelers of special status. They often apply to children and youth-student categories. On occasion, some airlines have also offered special consideration for seniors, the military, and clergy. The availability of these special-status offers varies by type of fare and, in some cases, by country of destination.

Families with special-status members therefore face even greater complexities of choice. For example, some types of low-cost fares, such as APEX, provide special fares for children, whereas others, such as most charters, do not. Thus, the total transportation bill for a family of two adults and two children might be lower with APEX than with a charter, even though the individual adult charter fares are substantially lower than APEX.

COMPARING CONVENIENCE

The two main factors in air-travel convenience are routes and schedules. You can't calculate a numerical convenience index, but you're obviously better off with nonstop or minimum-stop flights and convenient arrival and departure times. You might think it would be easy to evaluate these convenience factors, but even the terms used by the travel industry to describe the nature of a particular flight may not convey the realities you encounter.

Route Factors

First, a person might assume that a flight advertised as nonstop doesn't stop anywhere between the departure and arrival cities. But some airlines and tour operators may neglect to tell you that some supposedly nonstop flights from the West Coast can't make it to Europe without stopping for fuel at Bangor, for example. This problem is most prevalent with charters. Only under extremely rare conditions are the major airlines unable to keep their flights to truly nonstop schedules.

Most people might also assume that a direct or through flight connects two cities without change of plane. Again, a reasonable assumption isn't always correct. Airlines frequently apply a single flight number to what is actually a connection involving a change of planes. Where you have a choice, a genuine through or direct flight is clearly a better bet than one requiring you to gather up all your carry-on belongings, get off, go to another gate, line up, and get reseated—and finally resettled.

Not much can be misconstrued about connecting flights, and airlines tend to promote them accurately. Again, however, some connections are more tolerable than others. Most airlines try to minimize walking distance within gateway airports for connections with their own flights. For that reason, single-airline connections can be much more convenient than connections between two airlines, especially at the biggest U.S. airports. On the other hand, some charter programs involve a domestic flight within the United States on a scheduled airline to New York combined with a charter between New York and Europe. These connections often entail long distances between arrival and departure gates or terminals at Kennedy, and can require long layovers.

Schedule Factors

Schedule convenience is more subjective than some other convenience factors. Most travelers don't like to leave or arrive in the early morning; many find it inconvenient to have to leave or arrive during local rush hours. Beyond these obvious factors, however, traveler opinion seems to vary. Some travelers like to leave or arrive early in the day, others in the afternoon. Some travelers prefer day flying; others prefer to save vacation time by flying at night.

In any event, transatlantic travelers don't have much flexibility when it comes to schedules. Because of the combination of distance, flight time, and time-zone differences, most transatlantic schedules follow the same pattern:

- Eastbound flights leave the United States in late afternoon or early evening and arrive in Europe the following morning.
- Westbound flights leave Europe in late morning or early afternoon and arrive in the United States the same afternoon or early evening—thanks to a five- to eight-hour time-zone change.

Virtually all the airlines conform to this general pattern. It's convenient and efficient for the airlines. It's not so convenient for travelers: Every day planeloads of tourists arrive in European cities, often early in the morning and sometimes hours before the departing tourists have checked out of their hotels.

COMPARING COMFORT

Comfort depends mainly on two factors: how full your flight is and how roomy your seat is—considering both width and legroom. You might at first assume that neither of these comfort factors is subject to your control. Fortunately, you can do something about ensuring a relatively comfortable flight.

Load Factors

Frequent travelers know that there's nothing like an empty seat next to them to ensure a comfortable flight. Even a plane with the most overstuffed high-density seating is endurable when you can spread a few of your articles—and a few parts of your anatomy—into the adjoining seat. Personal service is also much better on flights with light loads. In fact, whenever you hear a frequent traveler proclaim that he or she had a "good flight," chances are that it wasn't more than about 60-percent full.

At least some of the time, you can increase your odds of an

uncrowded flight. You can choose to travel on a day when you'll be relatively sure of lighter-than-average loads. Midweek days are typically lighter than weekend days. Off-season is a better bet than peak season. In some cases, especially if you're booking near your departure date, your travel agent can check with the airline to determine which of several alternative flights will have the lightest loads. Don't hesitate to ask for this information either—remember that the airline would rather have you fly on a slow day than when it's booked solid.

Cabin Comfort

Infrequent travelers are often surprised to learn that all Economy Class airline seats don't provide the same amount of room. Certainly, you'd seldom find out from the airlines. Their promotions would lead you to believe that they all offer fabulous luxury in seating, but almost no carriers are really open and accurate about their seating standards.

In fact, there are substantial differences among various airlines in the width of seats and in the legroom they provide, which are strictly a matter of individual airline policy. By selecting one of the airlines that offers above-average comfort—or at least avoiding those that fly the worst "cattle cars"—you can do a lot to make your flight more pleasant.

Airlines' seat-width options are limited by the cabin dimensions of the planes. In general, the number of Economy Class seats per row in a wide-body airplane can fall into only one of two configurations; in a narrow-body plane, the number of seats per row is usually the same for all airlines.

The maximum Economy Class seat widths for the types of planes used across the Atlantic fall into four width groups, as indicated in table 1. Widths shown in the table are measured between armrest centers—indicative of the maximum side-to-side space available. Some airlines, however, use narrower seats in some or all locations, either to allow middle seats to be wider than outside seats, to provide wider aisles, or to make seating standard among different plane types.

Table 1   Maximum Aircraft Seat Widths

Aircraft type	Average number of seats per row	Maximum width (inches)
DC-10	9	20
L-1011	9	20
767	7	20
747	10	19.5
DC-8	6	19
DC-10	10	18.5
L-1011	10	18.5

Width differences of one-half inch are not trivial. When even the best Economy Class seating is very tight, only a half-inch less space for each of the nine or ten passengers in a row noticeably crowds everyone.

In most planes, a small number of seats provide substantially greater legroom than average or typical seats. Experienced travelers often ask for seats in rows by doors and emergency exits, for example, which normally have more space than those in the rest of the plane. Some travelers prefer bulkhead seats (the front row in a cabin)—many provide extra legroom, and even when they don't, there's nobody right in front of you to lean his or her seat back into your lap. On the other hand, bulkhead seats on some aircraft have tray tables built into the armrest; with thicker armrests, seats are narrower. Also, you often can't see the movie from some of these exit row seats, and many are right opposite noisy galleys. Travelers with babies are often assigned to the bulkhead rows. In any event, there aren't enough of these seats to go around. Your best bet is to choose a flight where seating throughout the plane is reasonably comfortable.

Front-to-rear space is important at two levels—literally. Legroom is obviously important. So, too, is chest-level room for reading, eating, and working. Front-to-rear space is measured by **pitch**, which is the interval at which seat rows are installed. Pitch is not governed by plane type; all modern commercial planes have seat tracks that allow airlines to adjust pitch in increments of one inch or less. The effective difference between the roomiest (36-inch) and tightest (30- and 31-inch) pitch is moderated through use of thin-back seats in the tighter installations. Compared with seats built, for example, 15 years ago, modern thin-back seats provide an effective legroom improvement of three to four inches. But airlines usually neglect to mention that their new thin-back seats do almost nothing to improve chest-level room. Moreover, most of their competitors with 33- or 34-inch pitch are also likely to be using thin-back seats if the seating is fairly new. While you'll probably find a new thin-back installation at 33 inches to be every bit as comfortable as the average Economy Class seating at 34 inches, you'll find 31- and 32-inch pitch noticeably more crowded, even with the thin-back seats.

Comfort is also affected by the seating configuration—the way seats are arranged in a plane. Any time you have to sit in a middle seat, with seats occupied on both sides, comfort is severely impaired for you and for the travelers seated on either side of you. Different seating configurations result in substantial differences in the percentage of total passengers whose comfort is diminished by occupied middle seats. Data on middle-seat occupancy shown in table 2 are based on an average load factor of 70 percent, with seats assigned to minimize the use of middle seats.

Table 2   Wedged-In Passengers

Configuration	Passengers adversely affected by middle-seat occupancy (percent)
2-2 or 2-2-2	0
2-3	21
3-3 or 3-3-3	50
2-3-2	15
2-4-2	18
2-5-2	20
2-4-3	30
3-4-3	47

Consumer Reports Travel Letter developed a composite seat-comfort index that combines the effects of seat width, pitch, and configuration into a single measure. Table 3 shows seating data, including the *CRTL* Comfort Index, for all planes flying the North Atlantic last summer. Substantial changes are not expected in 1988.

The Comfort Index was scaled so that the value for a DC-10 Business Class with eight-across seating at 36-inch pitch equals 100. This represents the most crowded seating that can truly be described as comfortable, even when the plane is full. Many Business Class planes are even less crowded.

Although no Economy Class seating is comfortable when the plane is full, you'll generally find that seating with indices in the range of 75 to 85 will meet reasonable expectations for seat room. In the range of 70 or 75 you'll feel noticeably crowded; you should avoid planes with indices in the 60s, if you can.

Table 3   Transatlantic Airline Seating

Airline	Aircraft	Seat pitch (inches)	Seat width (inches)	Seating across	*CRTL* Comfort Index
Aer Lingus	747	33	19.5	10	74
Air America[a]	L-1011	32	20	9	78
Air France	747	34	19.5	10	77
Air India	747	34	19.5	10	77
Air New Zealand	747	34	19.5	10	77
Alitalia	747	32	19.5	10	72
American	DC-10	33	20	9	80
American	767	32	20	7	78
Austrian	A300	32	19	8	73
Belair[b]	DC-10	32	20	9	76
British Airways[c]	747	36	20.5	10	86
British Airways[d]	747	33	19.5	10	74
Condor[b]	DC-10	31	18.5	10	64
Continental	747	33	19.5	10	74
Continental	DC-10	32	20	9	78
Delta	L-1011	32	19.5	9	75
Delta	767	32	20	7	78
EgyptAir	747	34	19.5	10	77
El Al	747	34	19.5	10	77
El Al	767	33	20	7	81
Finnair	DC-10	34	20	9	83
Hawaiian[a]	L-1011	32	18.5	10	67
Highland Express	747	33	19	10	72

Table 3   Transatlantic Airline Seating—*Continued*

Iberia	747	34	19.5	10	77
Iberia	DC-10	34	20	10	83
Icelandair	DC-8	32	19	6	69
JAT	DC-10	34	20	9	83
KLM	747	34	19.5	10	77
Kuwait	747	34	19.5	10	77
LTU[b]	L-1011	34	18.5	10	72
Lufthansa	747	34	19.5	10	77
Lufthansa	DC-10	34	20	9	83
Martinair[b]	747	32	19.5	10	72
Northwest	747	32	19	10	69
Olympic	747	34	19.5	10	77
Pakistan	747	34	19.5	10	77
Pan American	747	33	19.5	10	74
Piedmont	767	32	20	7	78
Royal Jordanian	747	34	19.5	10	77
Royal Jordanian	L-1011	33	20	9	80
Sabena	747	34	19.5	10	77
SAS	DC-10	34	20	9	83
Spantax[b]	DC-10	31	18.5	10	64
Swissair	747	34	19.5	10	77
Swissair	DC-10	34	20	9	83
TAP	L-1011	33	20	9	80
Tower[a]	747	34	19.5	10	77
TWA	747	32	19.5	10	72
TWA	L-1011	32	20	9	78
TWA	767	32	20	7	78
UTA	DC-10	34	20	9	83
Virgin Atlantic	747	31	19.5	10	69

[a] *Scheduled airline with extensive transatlantic charter service*

[b] *Charter airline*

[c] *Convertible Business-Economy cabins*

[d] *Economy cabins*

Other Comfort and Service Factors

Beyond seating standards, the other cabin-service elements that contribute to your overall flight comfort tend to be fairly subjective. Hot meal service at 40,000 feet may be a technological accomplishment, but the results seldom justify the efforts, at least in Economy Class.

Some travelers, of course, comment on the food as a key element of airline service quality. In reality, there's probably never been an Economy Class airline meal as good as what $6 will buy at your local diner. Obviously, then, the difference between the best and worst airline meals is, at most, a question of $2 to $3—hardly a figure on which to base a $1,000 ticket purchase. Maybe food looms important to many travelers because there's so little to do on a flight but eat.

Beverage and entertainment pricing is a more substantive criteria than food for choosing among airlines. When airline drinks sell for $3 or so and movie headset rentals are about $4, free drinks and/or entertainment are a substantially better reason than food quality for favoring one carrier over another. For 1988 travelers, quite a few major transatlantic airlines will offer free drinks and free headsets in Economy Class.

Airline in-flight surveys almost always show very high ratings for intangible service factors that reflect personal attention from ground and air staff—responses such as "friendly people" and "lots of personal attention" keep cropping up. That's easily understandable in such a people-oriented business. It's also such an intangible and variable factor that no objective consumer research and analysis can treat it. In most cases, load factor is the most important determinant of cabin-service quality: When the plane's not full, you get lots of friendly attention; when it's loaded, you're given minimal service. What happens to you is so dependent on the particular cabin staff assigned to your flight that there's simply no way to make an accurate prediction.

COMPARING CONTINGENCIES

Finally, you'll want to make some sort of assessment of your risk—what happens when there's a major foul-up, and how easy is it to recover? Although you could draw up an almost endless list of potential difficulties, five kinds of problems are the most likely:

1. flight cancellations, missed connections, or missed return flights
2. overbooking
3. lost baggage
4. personal illness or other emergency requiring predeparture trip cancellation or unscheduled early return after you're in Europe
5. becoming stranded due to operator failure

Some transportation options are more responsive to these problems than others. For example, at the top end of the scale, a First, Business, or full-fare Economy Class ticket on a major airline provides almost as much flexibility as having the price of the ticket as cash in your pocket. You can transfer these tickets among airlines at any time essentially at will.

At the opposite end, some cheaper options lock you into very inflexible positions. Specific differences are described in subsequent chapters.

DETERMINE YOUR PERSONAL BENCHMARKS

It's important to have your own benchmarks against which to measure the available options. Thus, no matter what form of ticket you decide to use or how you decide to buy it, you should use an APEX trip on one of the major airlines as the standard of comparison. To develop these benchmarks, simply find out from your travel agent or directly from one or more airlines:

- The APEX fare for your preferred route, for the time of year you intend to fly and on the days you want to travel. In comparing APEX fares, use as your benchmark the fare quoted by an airline that offers direct service between your city of origin and your European gateway. If you're traveling with children or others eligible for special-status fares, determine the total family cost for APEX, including any children's or youth fares that might apply.
- The best available schedule on a major airline: minimum total flying hours, whether nonstop flights are available, layover or connection times if applicable, and arrival and departure times.
- The comfort standards offered on the major airline(s) you're considering—in most cases, the majors will all offer standard seating.
- Your assessment of any contingencies you might face with an APEX trip on a major airline. Generally, risks of airline or operator failure will be minimal with this option, but the restrictions may pose a potential risk if you're likely to encounter last-minute changes in your travel plans.

This APEX trip will therefore be your benchmark. It will show you what you have to beat with any alternative you might consider. And if you can't beat the price, APEX is undoubtedly the way you'll finally travel.

USING THIS GUIDE

Obviously, this guide can't offer truly up-to-date airfare information for summer and fall 1988. The airlines usually don't know what the complex interactions of market forces, exchange rates, fuel prices, and government policies will bring six weeks in advance, let alone six months ahead.

The fare data in this guide can still be very useful to travelers planning 1988 European trips because:

- Estimated fare levels will be close to final figures, barring some major pricing upheavals.
- Relative fare levels—for the different types of service, to different European countries, from different parts of the United States, over different seasons—should probably be quite accurate, within a few percentage points. Any major changes should raise or reduce most fare levels in about the same relationship.
- The trade-offs between costs and the other important factors—convenience, comfort, and contingencies—should change little, if at all.

Travelers are urged to use this guide for general exploration of available options and to identify the specific questions that need to be asked. Then call or visit a travel agent as early as possible to get precise answers to your questions and exact costs. To ensure that you have the greatest likelihood of getting the best prices on fares as well as your first choices on dates and other specific arrangements, you should begin this process at least two months ahead of your departure date, if possible.

USING AND SELECTING A TRAVEL AGENT

Most travelers to Europe are probably better off buying their air tickets and tour packages from a travel agent rather than directly from an airline. Travel agents generally avoid the obvious biases of airline ticket offices in any questions that deal with airline choice. Typically, many travel agents can provide far more personal guidance about travel in general, and especially details about the various destination countries in Europe, than airline ticket-counter personnel. In addition, some of the more interesting airfare alternatives are available only through travel agents—you simply can't buy them directly from any airline. Travel agents provide convenient one-stop shopping for all your travel arrangements, including air tickets, rail passes, rental cars, and hotel accommodations. Now that most agents have reservations computers, they are also no longer at a disadvantage, compared with airline offices, in terms of immediate access to information and immediate confirmation of space.

Computerized reservations systems have done wonders for travel agents' efficiency. They permit virtually instant schedule information, space availability, and confirmation—not just for airline seats, but also for rooms in thousands of hotels, for rental cars, and for all sorts of other travel services.

But there is a downside to the computer story: Some agents may rely on the computers to such an extent that they are not prepared to deal with services not listed on the computer. And unfortunately, some of the very best airfare deals—even the relatively popular and well-known charters—are not listed. Moreover, although this book doesn't deal with hotels, note that the computer systems tend to include more of the higher-priced European hotels. More likely than not, budget hotel reservations are not available through computers here unless the hotels have U.S. representatives or belong to chains with U.S. reservations services.

Travel agents do not charge clients for making the most common and conventional travel arrangements. They earn their pay on commissions from the airlines, hotels, cruise lines, tour operators, and other suppliers. Commissions on most travel services generally run from 8 to 12 percent, but can be as high as 40 percent for some special services such as travel insurance.

You can't save money bypassing travel agents, at least on conventional travel services. Airlines, hotels, car-rental companies, and other suppliers typically will not sell directly to the public at net, no-commission prices.

Commissions are normally the agents' only income source. However, unless you're a very good year-round customer, you can expect an agent to ask you to cover any extraordinary costs your trip may entail, especially for last-minute reservations or changes that require extensive telephone or telex communications direct to Europe, or for extra rewriting or reissuing of airline tickets. The agent cannot recover these extraordinary costs from the suppliers, and agencies are therefore within their rights to ask customers to reimburse them. And of course, you'll be expected to cover any cancellation charges or refund penalties assessed by airlines or hotels.

Agents are not immune to the financial realities of the business world. As in any marketplace where agents' incomes are based on commissions, the more you spend, the more income your travel agent makes. Most agents resist trying to upgrade a typical bud-get-minded traveler from APEX to Business or First Class air ser-vice—perhaps because the price difference is so great that any such attempt would be absurd. But financial pressures might sometimes prejudice travel agents' advice toward APEX on a major airline and away from cheaper charter and bulk-fare deals, especially since the cheaper airfare not only reduces commission income but also, usu-ally, requires more work and therefore entails higher costs. So if you're interested in one or more of these low-priced options and your agent tries to steer you away from them, you should find another agent—one who knows about these deals and is willing to arrange them.

One other caution: On occasion, an airline might grant agents "override commissions" that are much higher than usual—perhaps up to 50 percent. The purpose is to get agents to book travelers on their flights rather than those of competitors. When big overrides are offered, some agents ticket their clients on itineraries that are clearly not in their clients' best interests, often explaining circuitous routings and connection delays as a consequence of lack of space on more direct services. But if your agent schedules you by what appears to be the long way around, make sure that either no better connections are available or the suggested schedule offers some substantial price advantage.

You certainly don't have to deal with a travel agent to get good travel counsel or to take advantage of some attractive rates. If you decide you'd rather deal with an airline than a travel agent, and you still want some personal guidance about your trip, visit one of the airlines' "vacation centers" in a major city. These airline offices are geared to provide much of the same kinds of travel information that you get from a good travel agent; people who staff them are usually far more informative than the often harried personnel in airline ticket offices or at airport desks.

The company you work for may have an in-house travel department. Although these offices are established primarily to arrange for business travel, many take care of employees' personal travel needs as well. Such travel offices can often arrange for you to enjoy the benefits of corporate rates and corporate discounts on your vacation trips.

How should you select a travel agent? First, you have to recognize that a big shakeout is occurring among travel agencies. Some are keeping abreast of the rapid changes in the travel marketplace of the late 1980s, while others are trying to turn back the clock and operate by 1970s rules. With airline deregulation have come a number of ways for travelers to minimize the prices they pay for individual travel services—specifically, to pay less than the sellers' official asking prices without any sacrifice in quality, convenience, or reliability. All these techniques are available to travel agents. You should view them as important items in a modern agent's "toolbox" of travel resources—alternatives that any agent should call upon to help clients get the best value. Specifically, any agent who wants to compete in the 1980s should be prepared to tap any or all of the following resources:

- discount airline tickets that can be sold to travelers at substantially lower prices than the airlines ask for the same tickets (see chapter 7)
- discount hotel accommodations, obtained through consolidators (see pages 66–67 and 168–69), tour operators, or consortium volume-buying programs, that can cut hotel costs by at least 20 percent at a large number of locations around the world

- frequent-flier airline coupons, obtained from coupon brokers, that can cut the costs of First Class and Business Class air travel by as much as 70 percent (see chapter 9)
- discount cruises and package tours, obtained either directly from the tour and cruise operators or from clearinghouses, which can cut 10 to 20 percent from a large number of cruises and tours—and cut prices even more for bookings made within a few weeks of departure

Agents who want to turn back the clock complain loudly about unethical competition from discount sources, but most consolidators, tour operators, coupon brokers, and clearinghouses are happy—even eager—to sell their services through travel agencies. Some agents also claim that discounters are unreliable. Certainly, a few discounters are unethical (more are ethical but undercapitalized, which may be worse), and some travelers have encountered trouble and lost substantial amounts of money in discount arrangements. But it's a serious breach of logic to conclude that all discounters are unethical and their discount arrangements risky. In fact, there are ethical and financially sound suppliers in all the discount groups—consolidators, consortiums, coupon brokers, and clearinghouses. Individual agents can serve their clients best by locating and using reliable discount sources rather than complaining about unreliable ones.

The travel-agency market seems to be evolving toward the same sort of stratification that has occurred in the securities market. Some inexperienced travelers may need advice and counsel throughout the entire travel-planning process, starting with the selection of places they want to visit. Like unsophisticated investors who rely on a stockbroker's research and recommendations, these travelers need a great deal of personal service and attention. This market is big enough to support a large number of travel agents who charge full commission on travel services sold at full retail prices. If you need this kind of help, by all means seek out a good full-service agency. The recommendation of a satisfied friend or business colleague is the best way to find one.

Experienced and knowledgeable travelers, like investors who do their own research, are interested mainly in efficient execution of orders at the best price, not in hand holding. They can logically expect their agents to obtain the very best prices available, including the discount prices that commonly exist for most travel services, most of the time, in most areas. If your friends or colleagues can't recommend such an agency to you, look for the small discount travel ads you find in the Sunday travel sections of most major newspapers, then call around to find out which one seems to offer the combination of services you require.

EXCHANGE RATES

All airfares quoted in this book are officially priced in U.S. dollars unless otherwise indicated. Some car rentals and rail passes are also officially priced in U.S. dollars, and dollar prices do not change as a result of changes in exchange rates.

Some car-rental rates and many surface-travel rates are officially priced in the local currencies of individual European countries. In this book, these prices have been converted to U.S. dollars *except* for local transportation costs in individual European cities, which are reported only in local currency. *Note*: Dollar conversions were calculated as of August 1987 and should be reliable for comparative purposes. Check for latest prices at current conversion rates when planning and budgeting.

2

Major Airlines

The term **major airline** refers to one of the large group of established companies that have been flying for decades. Majors based in the United States that provide transatlantic service are American, Continental, Delta, Northwest, Pan American, Piedmont, and TWA. The European-based transatlantic majors are Aer Lingus (Ireland), Air France, TAP–Air Portugal, Alitalia, British Airways, Finnair, Iberia (Spain), KLM (Netherlands,) Lufthansa (West Germany), Olympic (Greece), Sabena (Belgium), SAS (Denmark-Norway-Sweden), and Swissair. Their "major" status reflects both their long history and size. It also reflects exclusive membership in the International Air Transport Association (IATA) fraternity during precompetitive times prior to deregulation, as well as current participation in the various major airline fare-setting systems. These airlines almost always charge identical fares on the routes they serve jointly.

Although not based in Western Europe, Air India, Alia (Jordan), El Al (Israel), EgyptAir, JAT (Yugoslavia), Kuwait, and Pakistan are also majors and part of the worldwide system. These lines also have U.S. government authority to fly you from a few U.S. cities to several European gateways—almost always at the same fares as the other major lines.

Historically, these major airlines have attempted to offer a price and quality spectrum of air service appealing to all segments of the international travel market. They've certainly come close. For that reason, these lines have carried the overwhelming majority of transatlantic passengers, and they will again in 1988.

As indicated in chapter 1, the major airlines' primary approach to low-fare markets is to offer special Economy Class fares with restrictions that make them unattractive to business travelers. Often marketed as "discount fares" to the public, they are more correctly termed **promotional fares**.

All the major airlines' promotional fares are listed in the computerized reservations systems that travel agents use. These systems also specify restrictions and space availability. No travel agent should have any trouble determining the amount of the fare or how it can be applied.

ADVANCE-PURCHASE EXCURSION (APEX)

As discussed in chapter 1, the most popular promotional fares are those known as **advance-purchase excursions**, usually advertised as **APEX**. Some lines use other names for the same type of fare. Lufthansa calls it Holiday, for example. By and large, single airline APEX fares from major U.S. gateway cities to Europe are usually lower than connecting APEX fares from U.S. cities that do not have direct service.

A great deal of confusion about terms exists in the travel marketplace. *Promotional fare* is a term regularly used inside the travel industry, and is not generally used in dealings with customers. Instead, airlines tend to talk—erroneously—about their "discount fares" in ads and other sales materials. This distinction isn't just hair-splitting—real discount fares exist, and they're quite different from promotional fares.

Promotional fares are set by airlines at levels below "normal" full fares and are (usually) formally filed with the government or industry agencies that deal with such things. Most promotional fares are Economy Class, but promotional variations on First Class have occasionally been sold.

Discount fare should be reserved to describe tickets sold for less than the fare set by the airlines for any particular type of ticket. Again, true discounts are usually applied to Economy Class fares, but discounts are also available on some Business or First Class fares as well. True discount fares are described in chapter 7.

Typically, APEX fares have up to six main restrictions:

- advance purchase
- minimum/maximum allowable length of stay
- the implicit round-trip requirement
- prohibition against en route stopovers
- cancellation penalties
- capacity control, or arbitrary limitation on the number of seats on each flight that are sold at APEX prices

"Advance purchase" means that you have to make your reservations and purchase your tickets at a specified minimum time in advance of your departure date. Normally there is no maximum limit on advance purchase. In addition, some APEX rules require that tickets be purchased within a specified time period after you make reservations, regardless of how far in advance of departure.

Buying your tickets a long time ahead has both advantages and disadvantages. It's certainly an easy way to make sure that you get seats on the flights and dates you prefer—a real advantage if you plan to travel during peak periods. Early ticket purchase also usually gives you a hedge against possible changes in fares between the time you buy your tickets and your departure date. Although international airlines aren't required to do so, most of them "lock in" your reservation at the rate you paid. If fares are subsequently increased, your ticket price remains unchanged. If fares go down, the airline will refund the difference.

One disadvantage of early purchase is that you increase the chance of incurring a cancellation penalty if you have to change your plans or if you subsequently find a lower fare on some other kind of service (such as a charter) for which you are not entitled to a fare-reduction refund. You're also lending the airline money at no interest.

"One-way APEX" fares are available on a few routes and should be investigated if you're planning a lengthy stay abroad.

APEX fares on most routes from the United States to western Europe permit no en route stopovers, either at East Coast U.S. gateways or at intermediate European cities. A few APEX fares to some European points and to several cities in the Middle East do permit limited stopovers in western Europe, sometimes at extra cost. Only a very few APEX-type fares allow travelers from the interior United States to stop over in New York or some other East Coast gateway (see chapter 10).

Another restriction is that APEX fares are usually capacity controlled. This means that airlines can arbitrarily limit the number of seats they sell at APEX prices, on a flight-by-flight basis. The APEX allocation can be very small—even zero—during heavy travel times when managements believe those seats can be filled with higher-fare passengers. Even during more competitive times, APEX seats may sell out early on particular flights, leaving only higher-priced seats for late bookings.

Finally, most APEX U.S.-to-Europe fares provide reduced prices for children. The most typical formula is that children between two and eleven travel at two-thirds of the regular APEX fare. On some routes, children can fly for half the adult unrestricted excursion fare. This can be cheaper than two-thirds of an APEX fare. Check the options. Children under two go at 10 percent of the adult fare; but if the plane is full, they don't get a separate seat—you'll have to hold them. Details are discussed in chapter 11.

THE 1988 APEX FARE OUTLOOK

The airfare tables in chapter 11 show major airlines' peak-season APEX fares from four representative U.S. gateways to twenty-five gateways in western Europe and the eastern Mediterranean. Fares shown in the tables are those listed in airline computers (or obtained directly from airlines) as of summer 1987. The airfare tables also show effective dates and applicable restrictions.

Obviously, fares finally adopted for the 1988 peak season will differ. Even the airlines won't know exactly what they'll be charging for peak season until late spring. But the actual figures should be fairly close, and the relationships among different fare classes and fares on different routes should be very similar to those for peak 1987. A basic assumption in the use of summer 1987 fares is that there won't be many cost pressures on fares during the winter and spring of 1988.

Final 1988 peak-season fares will be a compromise between two offsetting economic forces:

1. Poor financial performance over the last few years by most major airlines will pressure them to increase revenues, mainly by increasing fares.
2. Increased competition from low-fare alternatives will put an effective lid on the fare increases that travel markets will tolerate.

The net result should be a minor increase in APEX and related major-airline fares this year.

CONVENIENCE

The major airlines provide nonstop, direct, and connecting flights to and from far more U.S. and European points than any other class of carrier does. In terms of convenience (and also contingencies, as discussed later) almost any nonstop flight is to be preferred over almost any direct flight or connection, regardless of other advantages and disadvantages.

The majors can't be beaten for schedule convenience, either. Wherever they arrive, flights on most routes operate every day. The most popular routes—for example, New York to London—may have up to ten daily flights; only a few, such as Seattle to London, may have fewer flights than one per day.

Major U.S. airlines will have direct service to Europe from many more U.S. cities than could possibly be included in any summary tabulation. You'd expect them to run more through-plane services from interior U.S. points than their European competitors, and they do. You might not expect that they also run direct flights to as many European cities as the European lines—or more. This is mainly because the U.S. lines typically run the same flight beyond its first European gateway to additional cities farther east, whereas European lines almost invariably require connections at their first-stop major gateway cities for services to other points.

But don't assume that through-plane service on the U.S. lines means that you won't have to change planes at some point. Some

airlines station small, short-range planes (727s and 737s) perma-
nently in Europe. The jumbo plane takes you to, say, London or
Frankfurt, where you change to the smaller plane for such cities as
Munich or Vienna to the east. Or on a flight operating from interior
U.S. points to Europe, you may start off your trip on a 727 or DC-9,
and change to a jumbo plane at an East Coast gateway. Unfortunately, these connections often carry the same flight number as
the transatlantic flight. So if you're about to choose what appears to
be a through flight with one or more intermediate stops, you might
check to see whether a "change of gauge" is involved—in the
United States, in Europe, or both—and select another airline if you
don't like the idea of changing planes.

COMFORT

All 1988 transatlantic service on scheduled major airlines will feature wide-body jets; 747s will predominate, with quite a few
DC-10s, L-1011s, and 767s. Seating data on all aircraft expected to be
used for transatlantic service are shown in table 3, pages 17–18. For
the most part, Economy Class seating will be comparable on most
major cities, with *Consumer Reports Travel Letter* Comfort Indices of
between 81 and 92.

One airline, however, provides substantially more room in
some Economy Class seats. Two of the cabins on British Airways
747s contain seats that can be converted on the spot to either Economy or Business Class, depending on the number of travelers in
each class on any flight. When used for Economy Class, seating is
nine across (instead of the normal ten), and pitch is 36 inches
(instead of the typical 33 to 34). Convertible seats in rows 17
through 26 are often allocated to Economy Class, and they provide
substantially improved comfort compared with conventional Economy seating. Unfortunately, British Airways normally doesn't pre-
assign these seats to Economy—they are given out, when loads
permit, only on the day of departure. So if you're flying British
Airways—and the substantially improved comfort is a good reason
to do so—you should check in early to be assigned (or reassigned)
seats in the convertible section.

A few years ago, several European-based major airlines
adopted a free-drink, free-headset policy. Now many airlines offer
free headsets and alcoholic beverages to Economy passengers. But

on some, expect to pay about $4 for a headset (to hear the audio programs and movie soundtrack), $3.50 for a drink, $3 for wine, and $2 for beer. Buying drinks and entertainment on those lines that charge for them could easily add $10 to $20 per person to the cost of a trip—enough to influence your airline choice. These policies change often, so ask about them.

CONTINGENCIES

Traveling with a major airline, even on the cheapest APEX, is probably your best insurance policy against the effects of Murphy's Law—"What can go wrong will go wrong"—on your trip. When equipment breaks down or weather across the ocean grounds the plane you were supposed to take, the majors, with their huge fleets and frequent flights, are better able to cope than are the smaller low-fare lines or charters. If your airline can't handle you, it can arrange for another major line to do so. If you and your baggage go separate ways, the majors can usually return it to you within a day or two. If you're denied boarding because of overbooking, you have specific—and sometimes very rewarding—recourse. (Overbooking rules also apply to low-fare airlines, but not to charter flights.)

Of course, your absolutely lowest-risk schedule option is a nonstop trip on a major airline. In fact, getting a nonstop flight is probably worth giving up something in the way of comfort or other advantages available only on through or connecting schedules.

If your route doesn't have nonstops, a true direct flight is almost as good. If you have to connect, same-airline connections are generally less risky than connections between different airlines. Minimum connecting times established by the airlines and published in the *Official Airline Guide (OAG)* are not long enough to provide slack in case a flight is late. Check the schedule to see whether an earlier flight can give you leeway to make your connection. You can usually find such a flight without having to pay the higher cost of a ticket that allows a stopover at the connecting city (a **stopover** is generally defined as four hours or more).

The majors have specific policies that entitle you not only to meals and accommodations if they keep you waiting because of a delayed or canceled flight, but to monetary allowances for immediate necessities if they lose your baggage. Remember, however, that accommodations are normally not authorized for delays at the airport where your trip originates. The presumption here is that you can just go home until things are fixed.

Major lines' APEX fares probably give you the best protection among the low-cost options against the technical and operational vicissitudes of flying. But you pay a price in flexibility. The airlines mean what they say about the restrictions. If you fail to show up for your return flight, you can't just get on the next one—you are no longer eligible for the APEX fare. Although your "busted" APEX ticket is still worth its cash value (less any applicable refund penalties), you have to exchange it for a higher-fare ticket to get home, an exchange that can cost you hundreds of dollars. Of course, if failure to make your scheduled APEX return flight is due to a delayed connecting flight, you'll be allowed to get on the next available return flight without penalty. This is not the case if for some reason you are traveling on two separate tickets: an airline completes its obligation when you get to the city shown on the ticket, even if you are late for another flight. Keep this in mind if you are traveling on a separately ticketed side trip and plan to fly into an airport just in time to meet your return flight on your APEX ticket.

If you miss your flight due to a medical problem or other documentable emergency, a letter from a qualified physician or government official (depending on circumstances) will normally permit you to reschedule your return without penalty.

Voluntary rerouting and rescheduling rules vary with the route. In most cases, any change (except an upgrade to a higher class of service) entails a penalty of $50 or, occasionally, 10 percent of the ticket value. Generally, you can retain the APEX price level (with penalty) if you change flights within the advance-purchase time requirement for new tickets. However, on a few routes, no-minimum-time reroutings and reschedulings are allowed, either free or for a set charge. If you think you'll change your plans after you're in Europe, you'll probably be better off with some more flexible low-fare option than APEX—for example, a one-way charter.

A few years ago, a guide such as this would have stated flatly that flying with a major airline is a 100-percent guarantee against getting stranded—a problem that still plagues charters. After several recent bankruptcies, however, such a statement would be rash in the extreme. In this deregulated environment, major-airline failure is a distinct, if distant, contingency. You can spot some dire warnings about airline solvency in the *Wall Street Journal*. It is possible, although unlikely, that another of the major U.S. carriers could cease operations in 1988.

You wouldn't be stranded if you were *in* Europe when the line on which you had a return ticket failed. The other major lines would almost certainly offer to fly you home without extra charge. And you can buy insurance that protects you in case of airline failure; ask your travel agent about such policies.

The possibility of major-airline failure should not deter you from traveling or from electing to use a major U.S. airline. This discussion is simply a recognition that the major lines have lost some of the lower-risk advantage they once enjoyed.

MAJOR AIRLINES' OTHER PROMOTIONAL FARES

APEX and its minor variants aren't the only promotional fares offered by the major airlines. Up to seven other types are available. Specific options vary with individual routes, as described in chapter 11.

Standby

Over the years, Standby has been used mainly for flights to London, but rarely for any other European capitals. Generally when you travel on **Standby**, you go to the airport the day you want to leave, get on a priority list, and wait until flight time. If any Economy Class seats are available after all the passengers with confirmed reservations have boarded, you get to go. If passengers with confirmed reservations fill the plane, you can try another flight, another airline, or another day. (Last year British Airways confirmed many flights for Standby passengers at its downtown ticket offices, as far ahead as nine or ten hours before departure.)

When Standby is available, it's often one of the most attractive alternatives. The fare is generally 80 to 90 percent of APEX. Of course, there is no advance-purchase restriction, and since it's a one-way fare, there is no minimum-stay requirement. In fact, Standby is often the only way you can fly one way on a major airline without paying the full Economy fare.

Standby offers excellent value. You fly on a major airline, with major line flight quality. Most direct U.S.-to-London routes offer at least daily service, and in the peak season there may be several alternatives every day. In most respects, it's a far superior alternative to a charter or to a multistop trip on a low-fare airline.

The obvious drawback is the uncertainty involved—you are not assured of a seat. However, dedicated Standby travelers from prior years report that Standby seats were a real problem only during a few of the very busiest weekends—eastbound mid-June through mid-July, westbound mid-August through mid-September, and around the Easter and year-end holiday seasons.

Youth Fares

Youth-fare tickets are available to travelers aged 12 through 24. On most routes, youth-fare tickets can be bought as one ways, round-trips, or open jaws. You can buy tickets at any time, but you can make reservations only within 72 hours of departure. Fares range from slightly lower to much lower than APEX; they're the same all year except to France, Portugal, and Switzerland, where peak summer one-way fares run approximately $20 higher than those for the rest of the year.

In 1987, year-round, one-way youth fares from Boston, New York, Philadelphia, and Washington to Amsterdam and Brussels were typically $169; to Frankfurt, Madrid, Munich, Stuttgart, and Zurich, $218; to Athens, Copenhagen, Milan, Rome, and Stockholm, $248. Fares from the West Coast were $100 higher; there were comparable add-ons from other U.S. cities. Youth fares to Paris were offered only on a round-trip basis, at $478 in summer and $438 the rest of the year.

The British government has not allowed youth fares, but the Standby program (when available) to London provides a good alternative.

Senior Fares

Only a few airlines offer fares to the senior market that are better than regular APEX fares. Two airlines offer 10-percent discounts to members of their senior clubs: American, on flights to West Germany; and TWA, on flights to Belgium, Israel, the Netherlands, and West Germany. Each club charges a $25 membership fee.

Holders of TWA's systemwide unlimited-travel senior pass

($1,399) can buy an add-on good for one transatlantic round trip for $422 (off-peak) or $522 (peak) as far east as Egypt or Israel.

Group and Tour Status Fares

Several types of group and tour fares are offered on various transatlantic routes. In most cases the actual fare levels are pegged at essentially the same levels as the least expensive APEX. However, restrictions and conditions of purchase can be quite different.

- **ITX** (inclusive-tour) and **GIT** (group-inclusive-tour) fares are designed as the airfare component of a complete tour package that also includes a mandatory minimum land package of hotel accommodations, sightseeing, and the like.
- **Incentive fares** cover programs organized by corporations, associations, etc., group travel to special events, or for group travel awarded for some achievement.
- **Weekend round-trip excursion fares** are offered from a few cities during fall, winter, and spring—allowing a maximum stay of only three or four days.

Some of these options aren't offered on all routes. Most routes have at least one of the three group, tour, or incentive options, but you can't buy them apart from a complete tour package.

ROUND THE WORLD

Most transatlantic airlines are involved in special Round the World ticket partnerships. For a set ticket price, travelers on most programs make as many stops as they wish, provided they keep going in the same direction—no backtracking—and stop only once at each stopover city. Of course, you can stop only at those cities served by the two or three airlines involved in the partnerships.

Many partnerships of a U.S. airline with one or two foreign lines have special Round the World fares. All offer Economy Class tickets, some offer Business Class, and most offer First Class options. Price levels depend mainly on the routing used to cross the Pacific. For travel via the North Pacific (including Honolulu), Round the World costs $2,100 to $2,600 in Economy Class, $3,000 in Business Class (where available), and $3,000 to $4,400 in First Class.

Travel via the South Pacific (including Australia, Fiji, New Zealand, and Tahiti) is several hundred dollars more.

In general, the first leg of the trip is treated as an APEX ticket—you have to reserve and buy tickets at least 21 days in advance. All the remaining legs can be left open if desired, usually for up to six months.

This program is obviously a good buy for people who want to go around the world. What may be a surprise is that it's sometimes the cheapest way to get to Europe, especially from the West Coast to the eastern Mediterranean. The reason is the availability of all those stopovers at no extra cost. Most of the cheapest promotional fares either permit no stopovers or only one, or two at best, to the eastern Mediterranean. So if you want to visit several different points in Europe and the United States as part of your trip, your standard alternative might be a very expensive full-fare Economy Class ticket or, even worse, a combination of individual-flight Economy tickets.

The best way to look at Round the World is as an absolute ceiling on what you should pay for an itinerary that involves multiple stops in internal U.S. and/or European cities. If you need a multistop trip, and if the regular Economy Class fare for that trip exceeds $3,100, Round the World can often serve as a cheaper alternative.

FULL-FARE ECONOMY

Full-fare Economy Class is the world's worst air-travel buy. You receive the same quality of service that you get on APEX at a much higher price. The only difference is the absence of restrictions— with full-fare Economy, you don't have to reserve or buy in advance, and you can buy one-way tickets.

But no sensible traveler should have to pay for full-fare Economy Class and still suffer Economy Class tight seating and service. If you're paying as much as full-fare Economy, you're probably better off paying a little more and moving up to the much better quality of Business Class. Or you could use one of the low-fare airlines that normally don't apply any restrictions, or buy a Business or First Class frequent-traveler coupon from a broker (see chapter 9).

BUYING YOUR TICKET

Obviously, the easiest of all tickets to buy are the majors'. Schedules, fares, and reservations are immediately available through the computers that are now installed in almost all retail travel agencies. You can use major credit cards to buy the tickets. It's as hassle-free as any big transaction can be.

3

Low-Fare Airlines

Low-fare airlines are scheduled airlines established specifically to provide low-fare, no-frills service. At this writing, it appears that at least four low-fare airlines will operate scheduled services between the United States and Europe this summer: Highland Express, Icelandair, Tower, and Virgin Atlantic.

THE 1988 OUTLOOK

You can look for slightly lower standard fares from the low-fare airlines plus, possibly, some short-term promotions at levels substantially below those of the major lines. In addition, the low-fare lines generally offer unrestricted fares at levels well below full-fare Economy on major lines. So if you decide to leave for Europe less than 21 days in advance, you should surely take a look at one of the low-fare options before you pay the huge premium for a last-minute ticket on a major line.

CONVENIENCE

Low-fare airlines have no inherent convenience differences from the major carriers. Travelers from the West Coast who use them have to change planes in Chicago, New York, or Newark, but that's simply because none of them carries enough traffic to justify nonstop service from the West Coast to Europe. There is nothing to prevent low-fare lines from applying for such service when the traffic warrants it.

Although it has no U.S. feeder service, Icelandair has organized special through-fare arrangements with several domestic airlines to feed its international flights from New York, Chicago, Detroit, and Orlando. Icelandair's European terminal in Luxembourg, although not one of Europe's major destinations, does provide easy access to some of the more popular cities, and the airline has developed some connecting services to facilitate through travel. For example, Icelandair operates free bus connections from Luxembourg to six cities in Germany, it subsidizes a low-cost train connection to any city in Switzerland or to Paris, and it also arranges for special connecting airfares to five other nearby European gateway cities. Most Icelandair flights stop in Reykjavik both ways, adding an extra two or three hours to the total trip from the United States to continental Europe, compared with competitors' nonstops to adjacent gateways. Icelandair has the authority to fly nonstop between the United States and Luxembourg but finds that most passengers prefer the Reykjavik stop, even if they don't stay over to tour Iceland.

COMFORT

Comfort standards on low-fare airlines vary from being comparable to the majors to substantially worse:

- Tower's 747s, with a *CRTL* Comfort Index of 77, and Highland Express's 747s, at 72, are similar to those operated by the major airlines.
- On planes flown by Icelandair and Virgin Atlantic, each with a Comfort Index of 69, you'll definitely notice more crowding.

CONTINGENCIES

Disruption of your travel plans is probably slightly more likely with a low-fare airline than with a major. Whenever any airline has to cancel a flight, its first-choice solution to the problem is to put you on another of its own flights. Obviously, it doesn't want to have to buy a planeload of seats from a competitor if it doesn't have to. Major lines can usually find enough seats on their own flights to cope with most cancellations; if not, the majors routinely accept each others' tickets and passengers, subject to applicable restrictions and space availability.

However, when a low-fare line has to cancel a flight, it may not be as likely to get you a seat on another line. Instead, it can ask you to wait, either for a replacement plane to show up or for available seats on one of its subsequent flights. If you're traveling with an airline that has only a few flights a week—and if bookings are heavy—you might have to wait a long time for another seat on that airline.

BUYING YOUR TICKET

Some schedules and fares for the low-fare transatlantic airlines are shown in travel agents' computers, but details are sometimes lacking. In practice, most agents call these airlines directly for current information.

4

Charters

Charters have traditionally offered the lowest airfares across the Atlantic. Their quality of service record is commensurately low. And despite much consumer-protection regulation, charters are still riskier than scheduled flights on either major or low-fare airlines. But tens of thousands of travelers use charters across the Atlantic every year, and probably most of them are repeat customers. They're satisfied with the product and more than satisfied with the price.

It's hard to generalize about charters. What counts is the individual charter you select.

TOUR OPERATORS

The main difference between a charter flight and an ordinary scheduled airline flight is that on a charter you buy your transportation from a wholesale tour operator rather than directly from an airline. The tour operator, in turn, contracts with an airline to fly you to Europe and back.

The critical distinction here is that your deal is with the operator, not with the airline. The operator is not an agent for the airline, as in the case of a retail travel agent. Instead, operators actually buy seats or entire flights for their own account. They "own" them and sell them for the best prices they can get.

Tour operators often charter planes from the world's biggest and best airlines—Pan American, United, Swissair, and the like. But these airlines normally don't offer the equivalent of a manufacturer's warranty. If you have trouble with the operator, you have to settle it with the operator, not the airline. It's somewhat like buying an article carrying a store's private label. If you have a complaint, you argue with the store, not the manufacturer.

This difference is critical to the existence of charters. It's the reason they can be cheaper than other kinds of flights, and it's also the root of almost all the problems that arise with charters.

1988 CHARTER FARE OUTLOOK

Charter fares are generally tied to scheduled airline fares by the marketplace, not by government regulation. Peak-season charter fares are usually $50 to $100 lower than major airline APEX round-trip fares to Europe from the East Coast, and $100 to $200 below APEX from the West Coast. You can expect about the same price difference this summer.

Charter fares, low-fare airline fares, and bulk fares (see chapter 5) between the United States and Europe tend to be quite close. Although substantial differences can exist on some routes at some times, these three different approaches to below-APEX fares on scheduled airlines are generally competitive.

Charter pricing is sometimes more finely tuned to the market than scheduled-airline pricing. Rather than having only two or three seasons, many tour operators offer a slightly different price on each flight. This way, the "normal" price difference can narrow in periods of the very highest demand and widen somewhat during slower periods. With fares varying every week, your round-trip price is the sum of one-half of the round-trip fares in effect for both legs of the trip. In fact, most charter programs now list fares in "half round-trip" terms.

Over the last few years most charter programs have offered one-way transportation as well as the more traditional round-trip transportation. One-way charter fares are typically $50 to $100 higher than one-half the round-trip fare. Tour operators with charters on more than one route usually allow open-jaw charters, with each leg priced on a half-round-trip basis.

Look for these traditional patterns to continue through the next year. No real innovations in charter fare offers are expected.

CONVENIENCE FACTORS

Charters don't have to be any less convenient than scheduled flights—but they often are. Basically, most charter programs are organized into weekly schedule patterns. Only a few of the most popular programs operate two or three times a week. This is not to say that charter flights to a particular European city don't operate more often, only that the flights of each specific wholesale tour operator seldom do.

Once-a-week operation can be a drawback for travelers with fixed vacation periods. If your vacation has to start on a Friday evening, and you have to be back at work on a Monday morning, using a weekly charter program with flights during the middle of the week could cost you a lot of time potentially available for your stay in Europe. Thus, for example, if you had to wait from Friday until Tuesday to leave, and had to come back on a Wednesday, three weeks off work would permit just two full weeks in Europe.

Incidentally, weekly charter-flight patterns also give a minor edge to U.S. charter airlines over European lines. Typically, a U.S. line starts its weekly round-trip with an overnight eastbound departure to Europe, returning westbound the following day. By contrast, a European line starts its round-trip with a daytime westbound flight to the United States, returning eastbound with an overnight flight the same evening. This pattern effectively provides an extra day in Europe on a U.S. carrier.

To see how this works, consider a one-week round-trip charter departing from the United States for Europe on a Saturday night and arriving Sunday morning. With a U.S. carrier, the return flight would leave Europe the following Sunday, allowing seven full days in Europe; with a European carrier, the return flight would leave the following Saturday, allowing just six full days in Europe.

Charter schedules can actually be more convenient than scheduled airline trips on a few routes. During the peak season, charters will operate nonstop from some U.S. cities (Cleveland and

Buffalo, for example) that do not have any nonstop scheduled-airline service. On the other hand, most charter schedules are no more convenient than those of scheduled flights, and many are less convenient. Scheduled flights from the East Coast generally operate nonstop to their European designations. Some charters, however, stop to board passengers from more than one East Coast gateway or drop people off at two or three European cities.

Quite a few charters from the West Coast involve stops or connections. Charter flights normally carry more passengers than flights on scheduled airlines, so some are simply too heavy to operate nonstop from California to Europe and have to stop to refuel in the eastern United States or Canada. Other programs feed charter flights departing from New York with passengers originating at many other U.S. cities, through connecting flights on domestic airlines, at special connecting fares. Although this kind of program brings charter service to many communities that could not support direct charter flights, the connecting times required in New York are often as long as four to six hours. Travelers on these programs are not allowed to switch to more attractive schedules for these domestic connecting flights.

Charter brochures often fail to mention extra stops or long layovers at connecting points. Travelers interested in finding nonstop or minimum-time flights should specifically check on stops or connections when comparing various charter alternatives.

One additional minor annoyance is that charter operators typically ask passengers to be at the airport for check-in three to four hours before departure, in contrast with the one hour that is advised by scheduled lines. And it's usually for "hurry up and wait" processing; there is often only one check-in position for 300 or so passengers.

COMFORT FACTORS

The most comfortable charters are generally the ones that use major-airline planes normally assigned to scheduled service. Seating on these is obviously the same as on scheduled service; on most, you can enjoy the added comfort of Business Class or First Class seating at nominal extra cost (see chapter 8). But most charters use planes specifically outfitted for charter service, with all-Economy seating. The best of these are usually 747s, with the standard ten-across seating and pitch equal to or slightly below that of scheduled major airlines.

Finally, several big charter programs that would otherwise be among the best use the least comfortable planes. Charter-style DC-10s and L-1011s typically combine narrow ten-across seats with 31- and 32-inch pitch. Any time you find charters with 370 to 380 seats on DC-10s and L-1011s, you know the seating is ultratight. Sardine-can crowding detracts from the otherwise excellent services found on Condor (DC-10) and Spantax (DC-10), whose *CRTL* Comfort Indices are as low as 64.

CONTINGENCIES

Charter programs involve two contingencies not associated with flights on major airlines: program cancellation and operator failure. Program cancellation is the less troublesome of the two. In recent years, charter markets have been sufficiently soft that several widely advertised programs have been canceled entirely or severely curtailed. As long as the operator remains solvent, however, this situation doesn't necessarily mean big trouble for travelers:

1. In many instances, an operator who doesn't sell enough seats on a charter program to make it pay simply cancels the charter and cuts a deal with a major airline to accept the few travelers who did buy charter tickets. Travelers in this situation often enjoy a better flight than they expected, on a major airline at the charter price. In fact, some large charter operators regularly use this technique to extend their season. Knowing that early and late bookings won't be enough to fill a DC-10, for example, Condor may buy space on Lufthansa for these dates rather than operate its own plane half-empty.
2. Even if the operator doesn't arrange an alternative, as long as the company stays in business, you'll get a refund. Your main worry may be finding replacement space after a late cancellation of a charter program.

Operator or airline failure, on the other hand, can be a disaster. The specter of tour-operator and airline failure has haunted the U.S. charter industry since its inception. Fear of being stranded has made charter travel an unacceptable alternative for many cautious travelers. Fortunately, there haven't been any major tour-operator failures in the last two years to strand charter passengers in Europe. But a couple of years without a significant failure in Europe doesn't eliminate the risk for 1988.

As mentioned, a successful charter purchase requires performance on the part of two separate suppliers, the wholesale tour operator from which you buy your seats and the airline that actually provides your travel services. If either supplier drops the ball, you're in trouble. Depending on circumstances, either an operator failure or an airline failure can strand you, delay you, or cause you to lose the money you paid for a charter flight.

Airline failure is usually a less severe problem than operator failure. If an airline fails, the operator normally still has your transportation money and can make deals with other airlines to operate your trip. What happens to you, the traveler, depends on which stage of your trip you're on.

The worst case occurs when you're already at your destination and about to come home. You'll probably have to wait there while the wholesale tour operator finds a plane from another charter airline or some extra seats on a scheduled airline.

If an airline fails just before the trip is scheduled to begin, you face a possible delay of days or weeks while the operator arranges alternative airline space. If you can't live with the new schedule, federal regulations require that you get your money back in full— but of course, you miss the trip. On the other hand, if the failure occurs several weeks or months before your trip is due to start, you might not even notice its effects. The wholesale tour operators can usually find a replacement charter airline within that time.

Operator failure is usually much harder on the travelers involved. Operator failure often means that some or all of the money earmarked for airline payment is gone. The operator has somehow obtained access to it and diverted it to other uses. Without any source of payment, airlines are not obliged to take you anywhere— or bring you back from where they already took you.

Charter passengers theoretically have two government-required safety nets to prevent monetary loss: Tour operators must post a performance bond; and passengers' prepayments are supposed to be placed in trust or escrow accounts, to be used only for payment for air travel. Certainly, these protections have decreased consumer problems with operator failure. But the safety net clearly has some gaping holes in it. Airlines and operators still fail, and travelers are still stranded. Many travelers find that extra-cost trip-interruption insurance is the best protection against potential problems. You can buy it through your travel agent when you book your charter.

Charters are the best deals on many routes, and travelers do not have to take unacceptable risks to enjoy their benefits. Here are some ways you can avoid—or at least minimize—your chances of being stranded or losing your prepayment:

1. Look for programs that use charter airlines with demonstrated records for reliability. The biggest foreign-flag charter carriers are Air Charter (France), Balair (Switzerland), Condor (Germany), LTU (Germany), Martinair (Netherlands), and Spantax (Spain). They either are affiliated with major scheduled carriers or are large independent corporations with extensive intra-European schedules as well as transatlantic services. Your travel agent should be able to advise you about the airlines used in any charter program.

2. Look for tour operators with a demonstrated track record for reliability. Probably the safest bets are those wholesale tour operators that are affiliates of top European charter airlines: DER Tours (Condor) and German Charters (LTU) come to mind as among the most stable. But quite a few independents have also developed good reputations: Council, GWV Travel, Wainwrights, Travac, and Unitravel are among the larger tour operators based in the United States with charter programs from major cities all around the country, and many more operate regionally or from single U.S. cities. Unfortunately, even a good 15-year track record doesn't assure future performance. Your travel agent should make special inquiries in the trade about how the operator he or she may have used satisfactorily in the past is doing at the time you're booking your charter.

3. If you have a choice, buy a charter on a program that shares a large plane with several different wholesale tour operators' programs. That way the failure of a single operator won't require the entire flight schedule to be canceled.

4. Make sure that your check (if you buy direct) or your agent's check is made out to the escrow or trust account established

for each charter program. This protection is required by the U.S. government of all charters; yet operators report that more than half the checks they receive are made out to them, rather than to those special accounts. Any charter traveler who makes a check out to a tour operator rather than an escrow or trust account is voluntarily giving up the security available for her or his investment.

5. Buy through an accredited travel agency. In bailout situations, the industry has tended to provide more help to travelers who bought their tickets through agencies than to those who bought directly from a defunct airline or tour operator.

Despite all your best pretrip efforts, you can still get stranded. Probably at least one charter program will strand its passengers within the next year. If you do find yourself at the airport ready to come home, and your promised plane doesn't show up, get all the information available about what is happening.

Unless you are assured of a quick fix, you should immediately face your most important question: How long can you wait for a solution that doesn't require you to pay anything extra? It could easily take up to 48 hours before you have the full story, and you may have to wait a week before your charter airline or tour operator can implement a rescue operation at no cost to you.

If you can't accept a delay of one to three days, you may as well resign yourself to extra cost and start shopping for a new ticket home: one way on a low-fair airline, Standby (if available), or a seat on some other charter. But if you take this sort of initiative to get back the quickest way, you'll have to pay separately, with little chance of a refund.

If you decide you can wait a day or two, you can expect some sort of bailout to be organized. If you're lucky, either the tour operator or the airline (whichever did not fail) will have a representative at the airport to keep you informed and to help with whatever arrangements are offered—alternative flights, interim accommodations, meals, and the like.

You may not find anyone at the airport who knows anything about what has happened. This situation arises at airports where your charter airline doesn't have its own personnel, where the airport itself or some other airline normally handles check-in and boarding. If that is the case, and unless you're out of funds, it's probably a good idea to check in to an airport-area hotel, to have a place where people can contact you. Even if you don't get reimbursed, or even if you don't stay all night, it's good insurance. If possible, have at least one person in your party stay at the airport for late developments and have one member remain accessible to a telephone.

Then telephone some friend or relative at home who can contact the wholesale tour operator's home offices in the United States (in case of an airline failure) or your retail travel agent (in case of a tour-operator failure) to find out what's going on and what you should do. Someone at home can be far more effective than you can be from Europe.

Almost all of the U.S. charter airlines and tour operators will likely provide reliable service this year. But the unfortunate fact is that many of them are undercapitalized and vulnerable to failure. Unless you are very confident of the operator and operator's airline, include the cost of trip-interruption insurance (about 5 percent of the ticket price) when you compare the prices of transatlantic airfare alternatives.

BUYING YOUR TICKETS

Charter-flight tickets are sold only through retail travel agents. You cannot buy them directly from a charter airline. Most wholesale tour operators have subsidiary retail outlets, and they often encourage travelers to buy through these subsidiaries. However, any travel agent can obtain charter tickets for you, at standard prices, and earn standard commissions in the process.

Charter-flight schedules and fares are not contained in agents' computerized reservations systems. To get the necessary details agents have to rely on brochures and telephone calls to charter operators. Therefore, some of the less enterprising travel agents tend to ignore charters. It's much easier for them to sell you a major-line APEX or a low-fare airline ticket. Any travel agent can sell you a charter, but finding an agent who will take the time to get details for you is a matter you will have to investigate for yourself.

The terminology of charter travel is sometimes confusing. Organizations that operate charter-flight programs are called "wholesale tour operators," whether or not the flights include complete tour packages. In fact, most of the operators that run charter programs also offer optional complete tour packages as well, but even if they run only charter flights, they're still called wholesale operators.

5

Bulk Fares

Bulk fares are a boon to budget-minded travelers. They can under-cut round-trip APEX transatlantic major-airline fares by as much as $200, without any sacrifice in service quality.

Bulk fares work quite simply. One airline might find that its bookings are slow for a particular period. Another airline might want to start a new European route from a U.S. city that hasn't had nonstop service before, but is unsure that it can sell enough tickets to fill the planes. A third airline might foresee substantial excess capacity on some routes, while a fourth airline is hard up for cash and needs assured revenues. For these and other reasons, airlines may decide to sell large numbers of seats in bulk to tour operators who will, in turn, market them to the public. The tour operators, often the same ones who run charter programs, commit for the space, and perhaps even pay in advance. It's then the tour operators' job to sell those seats, and they do it by cutting prices.

Bulk-fare deals can be made on either major or low-fare air-lines. Some big wholesale tour operators that once ran large charter programs have switched almost exclusively to bulk-fare programs. In fact, it is sometimes hard to tell the difference between charter, bulk, and discount fares.

In chapter 4, an analogy was drawn between the purchase of charter fares and the purchase of a private-label article: Your deal is with the retailer, not the manufacturer, and if something goes wrong your only recourse is to the retailer.

With bulk fare, the analogy is to buying a discounted brand-name product under warranty. Once you have bought it, the manufacturer is responsible, no matter what might happen to the retailer.

THE 1988 FARE OUTLOOK

Bulk fares look like one of the best opportunities for you to cut your transportation bill in 1988. These special fares should be available on most key transatlantic routes. Look for prices that are about $50 to $100 below APEX from the East Coast and $100 to $200 below APEX from the West Coast for comparable periods.

Bulk fares will theoretically be available all year. But your best deals will obviously be in the low and shoulder seasons (see page 10), when many airlines will be eager to add to their otherwise low revenue base.

CONVENIENCE

There are no inherent convenience differences between bulk-fare travel and regular-ticket travel on the same airline. However, the way airlines offer bulk fares may introduce some convenience differences.

Bulk fares are used, for example, to beef up traffic on schedules that aren't competitive. Whereas people willing to pay full APEX fares could be nonstop on some airlines, the lower bulk price compensates for the disadvantage of stops and plane changes for many bargain hunters. Bulk fares are also used to attract travelers through some of the less-used gateways in North America.

Certainly not all bulk fares entail less than nonstop convenience. Several of the biggest major carriers will almost surely negotiate peak-season bulk-fare deals on nonstop flights from many U.S. cities to Europe in 1988.

There aren't any standard restrictions on bulk fares. Specific ticket conditions depend on the deals struck between individual airlines and tour operators. Bulk-fare tickets normally have fewer restrictions than APEX; many don't have any. If there are restrictions, the most likely one is a minimum stay. Since tour operators want as much time as possible to sell, advance-purchase requirements are uncommon with bulk-fare tickets.

Some bulk-fare tickets are limited by season or by day of the week or are sold only for specific flights and dates; others are good for any available flight. There may not be a wide selection of bulk-fare seats during the very peak of the season.

Finally, the bulk-fare market is more fluid than the normal APEX market. Some bulk-fare deals are established months in advance for an entire season. But others come up suddenly, for example, if a certain airline runs into a slow period or competition pushes too much capacity on an individual route. Accordingly, you won't know exactly what bulk fare is available for any given period until closer to the dates you may want to travel. For that reason, reliance on bulk fares might be a little more of a gamble in terms of scheduling your trip for maximum economy.

COMFORT

Nothing in bulk-fare travel is inherently more or less comfortable than travel with any other form of ticket. Since bulk-fare deals are available on scheduled major airlines and low-fare airlines, comfort and service standards on the average are apt to be as good as charter standards or better.

But comfort depends on the airline, and some scheduled major and low-fare airlines' service levels are actually below those of a few of the better charter lines. If you're considering the bulk-fare option, your first consideration is the airline you'd be taking. Check the data on comfort and service quality for that line in chapters 2, 3, and 4.

CONTINGENCIES

One of the best advantages to the bulk-fare alternative is that it provides better protection against operator failure than a charter.

With a bulk fare, your transportation contract is with the *airline*, not—as in the case of a charter—with a wholesale tour operator. The airline is responsible for getting you home. The main risk element in bulk fares is that you're totally tied to the airline and operators involved in issuing the tickets. Typically, your bulk-fare ticket will have an endorsement indicating that it is valid only on the issuing airline and cannot be transferred to another.

Accordingly, if your flight is canceled or delayed, you can't take your ticket and expect to get on some other airline's next flight. Still, a bulk-fare ticket is probably no riskier than an APEX ticket. In either case, the airline will obviously put you on its next available flight. When the issuing line is clearly at fault, as for a missed connection, it may well endorse your ticket over to another line anyhow (if the other line has space available), even though it then loses the revenue from your trip.

BUYING BULK FARE TICKETS

Bulk fares are not as widely available as regular APEX or low-fare airline tickets. They are not in the airline reservations computers most travel agents use, they are not available directly from an airline through the ticket offices, and you can't buy them at the airport.

Instead, bulk-fare deals are normally handled by the same people who organize charters (see chapter 4). These people are already set up to distribute low-priced airline tickets. They make the basic agreements with airlines and sell some seats through their own retail subsidiaries and the rest through other retail travel agents.

To travelers, the distinction between bulk fare and charter may appear to be more of an obscure legal nicety than a a significant factor. In fact, the distinction is important when something goes wrong; you're generally better off with a bulk-fare deal than with a charter.

Wholesale tour operators in the United States still tend to be small. Many are active in only one major U.S. metropolitan area; a few of the larger ones may operate regionally. They generally advertise in local newspapers that serve their market areas. Your best bet to find out about which wholesalers are offering bulk deals—and which travel agents are handling them—is to read the weekly travel sections of your metropolitan newspapers, usually in the Sunday edition.

In their promotional materials, wholesale tour operators often don't make a clear distinction between their charter offerings and their bulk-fare deals, and prices are often comparable. So if you're looking at options, you have to ask specifically which of the low-fare specials are charters and which are bulk fares. You also have to ask specifically about schedules (check especially on the possibilities of extra stops or changes of plane). And you have to ask about the specific airline, so you can evaluate the comfort and quality standards.

In a few programs, the operators may not know early in the season whether any given flight and date will be operated with a charter or a bulk-fare deal. Even when they accept your reservation, they may retain the option of arbitrarily assigning you to either a charter or a bulk-fare deal, depending on how many tickets they sell and the deals they subsequently make with airlines. The normal contracts allow operators this flexibility. So if you want to guarantee a preferred option, you should insist on supplementary written assurance that your trip will be as initially specified. If the operator won't give such assurance, find another operator, or be prepared to accept a lower-quality option than you originally expected.

It's also sometimes hard to tell the difference between bulk and discount fares (see chapter 7). Many tour operators who sell bulk-fare tickets are also consolidators who sell discount tickets.

Despite somewhat greater uncertainties than on APEX tickets, bulk-fare tickets represent a tremendous opportunity to cut your transatlantic transportation bills. Many will find the minor drawbacks more than offset by prices that are as much as $200 below the usual options. On the average, a bulk-fare deal probably represents an alternative slightly superior to a charter flight, at about the same price. You can look for a very big year for bulk fares.

6

Last-Minute Travel

If you can afford even the slightest flexibility in your travel plans—
in terms of the dates of your trip, the city from which you originate,
or your destination gateway city—you can often fly to Europe at a
substantially lower cost than on any firm-schedule option. Being
flexible doesn't mean keeping your suitcase by your bedside at all
times, awaiting a call that sends you racing to the airport. Instead,
it means some combination of willingness and ability to:

- delay making your final arrangements until a few weeks before you leave
- remain uncertain about your exact flight date and schedule
until a week before you depart
- accept a flight to some European city other than your preferred destination
- conform exactly with someone else's travel plans

Quite a few different kinds of travel-marketing organizations have
sprung up in recent years to sell various types of last-minute travel.
Basically, they all provide outlets for airline seats (as well as cruise
cabins, tours, and hotel rooms) that would almost certainly remain
unsold through retail travel agents. These organizations market
this excess capacity in much the same way tickets to Broadway

shows that remain unsold by the day of performance are marketed at half price by special agencies like the one in Times Square.

The airlines and tour operators prefer to use relatively anonymous marketing organizations to sell off their excess capacity. That way they can keep trying to sell at full price through retail travel agents.

"GENERIC" AIR TRAVEL

A few travel-marketing organizations specialize in what can be described as generic air travel. This air travel is on fully government-certified and approved airlines, but with no prior "brand" (airline) identification. You never know which airline you'll be flying until you see the plane at the airport. Last year, generic travel pioneer Airhitch charged $160 each way from major northeastern airports (Boston, New York, and Washington); $229 each way from the Midwest, Texas, and Denver; and $269 each way from the West Coast. To use this service, you register with a fee (approximately $25) that is applied toward the ticket cost; you indicate a range of departure dates and a preferred destination gateway city in Europe. Then, about five days before the beginning of the indicated date range, you call a toll-free number to find out what flights will probably be available. You are notified of one or more flights, with dates and departure times, for which you should stand by. At that time, you send in the remainder of the cost and receive a voucher for the flight in the mail. Then, on the designated date, you go to the airport and check in as an Airhitch standby. If seats aren't available, you stand by for the next flight, possibly the same day, more likely the next. If no seats are available during the entire departure-date range, you get a refund. However, Airhitch reports that at no time last year did a week pass without enough seats to Europe to satisfy the demand. Return flights, at the same cost and on the same basis, are arranged with affiliated offices in Europe.

According to the generic travel organizations, about 90 percent of these flights to Europe arrive at airports within a 300-mile radius of Brussels. The main gateway airports are London, Amsterdam, Brussels, Frankfurt, Geneva, Madrid, Milan, Munich, Paris, Rome, and Zurich.

Flights can be on major airlines, low-fare airlines, or charters. Last year the mix was about half scheduled airlines and half charters. Of course, you don't get your choice; you either take what is offered or lose your fee and your place in line.

Moreover, this approach has some risks. It's basically a form of Standby but operated by an outside organization rather than individual airlines. As such, it does not guarantee a seat. And even if you get a seat, a trip to London isn't always an acceptable alternative if you really want to go to Paris, Zurich, or Rome. Getting from where you arrive to where you really want to go could more than eat up the possible fare savings—and add as much as two extra days of arduous land travel. Other costs not to be overlooked may be travel expenses—whether bus, train, or taxi fares or parking for a car—for more than one trip to the airport if you don't make a flight on your first day. Also consider the expense of an overnight stay in your departure city if you live elsewhere and can't return home if your standby carries over to a second day.

The other main drawback is that you may well wind up on one of the very lowest-quality services—a three-stop, twenty-hour endurance test on flights from the West Coast, or a densely packed seating configuration that might prove excruciating. Operators concede this risk. The system is intended for travelers who care more about price than about quality.

On balance, it would appear that this type of travel is best suited to the youth/student market. Other travelers with a youthful outlook—and more time than money—will also find it attractive.

LAST-MINUTE-TRAVEL CLUBS

Last-minute-travel clubs have recently received extensive publicity. Although most of the offerings available on a last-minute basis consist of complete tour packages and cruises, some air-only trips are offered. And the complete tour packages are often good deals at the reduced prices—even if they aren't especially good deals at their regular prices.

The mix of tours offered through last-minute-travel clubs mirrors the main focus of the regular tour market. Most of the activity to Europe is during the summer, although some popular destinations are offered year-round.

Last-minute prices represent cuts of 20 to 50 percent off list prices on most tours and flights. As might be expected, the price cut tends to be inversely related to the number of selling days left before departure.

Typical lead times for last-minute tours and flights range from a few days to a few weeks. A sampling of offerings last summer indicated that most of the tours sold at any one time were for departures within one to four weeks of the times they were announced. In a very few cases, departures were offered on an all-year or all-summer basis.

A few organizations indicated that special prices were also available for other travel services, such as rental cars and hotel rooms. These, however, were not listed in any of the bulletins or the hot-line messages; you had to make a special request to obtain them.

Most last-minute-travel marketing organizations operate as clubs. Travelers have to join officially and pay dues before they are eligible to purchase travel services. These clubs will enroll you and sell you tickets at the same time.

Clubs handle communications with their members in two ways. Some use recorded toll-free hot-line telephone messages. Other prefer to use printed listings in the form of bulletins.

Most last-minute-travel clubs are in the eastern United States and the Midwest. Most of the flight and package tours to Europe they offer originate in the East or Midwest as well. A disproportionate number of tours and flights sold in all markets depart from New York, reflecting the travel industry's traditional overuse of this gateway.

The West is a different area in which to find last-minute tours. Most marketers indicated that West Coast airlines and tour operators don't have enough excess capacity to provide a viable market. There are, however, ways around this problem. For example, clubs can arrange for California passengers to use a low-fare airline to connect with last-minute tours and flights departing from Chicago, Miami, and New York.

Indeed, the main caveat in last-minute-travel purchase is the limitation in departure-city options. You might find a spectacularly good deal on a tour departing from New York that exactly suits your needs. But the costs of buying separately ticketed transportation from your home city to New York and back could easily wipe out your savings, compared with a list-price tour or a flight that departs directly from your home city or one that permits a low-cost add-on fare to New York.

COMPANION TICKETS

All the major domestic airlines in the United States operate some sort of frequent-flier program. These programs offer a mix of awards to enrolled members, based on accumulated mileage logged on the sponsoring (or affiliated) airlines. Awards can range from a free upgrade from Coach to First Class, to unlimited free systemwide travel for a month. Some of these programs specifically offer awards that include travel benefits for members' companions. Enterprising frequent travelers can opt for these companion awards and then sell the companion ticket to anyone willing to pay their asking price.

This practice is perfectly within the airlines' frequent-flier-program rules. Your main limitation as a buyer is that you have to conform your trip to the schedule of the person from whom you buy the companion ticket. Most programs require that companions use the same flights, at least for the outbound portion of a round-trip. With some programs, you also have to make your deal far enough in advance to have the companion ticket issued by the airline in your name.

Price levels depend strictly on what the seller thinks he or she can get and what the buyer is willing to pay. In other words, they're subject to individual negotiation. One ad, for example, offered a First Class round-trip companion ticket from San Francisco to Germany for $600, surely one of the best travel deals of all time.

Companion travel is especially attractive for single travelers. Acquiring a companion ticket from a frequent-flier participant potentially offers a great savings, at least in terms of last year's typical asking prices. The main problem is, quite simply, that the total number of these opportunities during the year is probably measured in the hundreds, compared with millions of people who want to travel. Still, there's no harm in keeping your eyes on the classified travel ads.

BUYING LAST-MINUTE TRAVEL

Generic flights are available only from a few companies:

Airhitch
2901 Broadway, Suite 100
New York, NY 10025
212-864-2000
Deposit: $25

Access International
250 West 57th Street, Room 511
New York, NY 10019
212-333-7280
Deposit: None

Several organizations offer last-minute flights and tours:

Adventures on Call
Box 18592
BWI Airport, MD 21240
301-356-4080
$49 per family

Discount Travel International
The Ives Building, Suite 205
Narberth, PA 19072
215-668-2182
$45 per family

First Travel Club
955 American Lane
Schaumburg, IL 60173
312-240-2626
$48 per family

Last Minute Travel
132 Brookline Avenue
Boston, MA 02215
800-527-8646 (617-267-9800 in MA)
$30 per person, $35 per family

Moment's Notice
40 East 49th Street
New York, NY 10017
212-486-0503
Also 1750 112th Street N.E., Suite B112
Bellevue, WA 98004
800-235-5800 (206-453-1180 in WA)
$45 per family

On Call To Travel
14335 S.W. Allen Boulevard, Suite 209
Beaverton, OR 97005
503-643-7212
$39 per person

Quick Trips International
50 North Broadway
Palatine, IL 60067
800-558-1199 (312-359-1774 in IL)
(Available at variable charges through participating travel agencies)

Sears Discount Travel Club
Dept. 404, 311 West Superior Street
Chicago, IL 60610
800-331-0257 (800-826-4398 in IL)
$45 per family

Encore/Short Notice
4501 Forbes Boulevard
Lanham, MD 20706
800-638-8976
$48 per person for Encore, $36 for Short Notice

Stand-Buys Ltd.
311 West Superior Street, Suite 404
Chicago, IL 60610
800-255-0200 (800-826-4398 in IL; 312-951-7589 in Chicago)

Trans National First Service/Last Minute Traveler's
2 Charlesgate West
Boston, MA 02215
800-342-5682 (617-262-9205 in MA) for First Service
800-262-0123 for Last Minute Traveler's
$29 per person, $39 per family for First Service
$9 per person for Last Minute Traveler's

Travelers Advantage
831 Greencrest Drive
Westerville, OH 43081
800-835-8747
$39 per family

Up 'n Go Travel
10 Mechanic Street
Worcester, MA 01608
800-521-0103 (800-527-7710 in MA; 617-792-5500 in Worcester)
$40 per family

Vacation Hotline
1501 West Fullerton Avenue
Chicago, IL 60614
800-423-4095 (312-880-0030 in IL)
No fee

Worldwide Discount Travel Club
1674 Meridian Avenue
Miami Beach, FL 33139
305-534-2082
$35 per person, $50 per family

Companion travel tickets are normally obtained directly from the individuals who earn these awards. Individuals with companion tickets to sell generally advertise in the classified sections of major newspapers, under "Travel," "Tours," "Transportation," or "Tickets" headings.

7

Discount Tickets

Real discount air tickets were defined in chapter 2 as tickets sold for less than the airlines say those tickets should cost. Ticket discounting is wide open for flights across the North Pacific; nearly everyone seems to be able to arrange for discount prices 20 to 30 percent below the airlines' lowest promotional fares.

Ticket discounting is considerably less active for travel to Europe than to Asia. Still, more and more discount tickets are coming into the marketplace. It's important for travelers to know about them—what they are, how they work, and who sells them—whether or not they decide to buy them.

DISCOUNTING—HOW IT WORKS

True discounts on airline tickets reach the marketplace in three main forms: consolidator discounts, indirect rebates, and agency discounts.

Consolidator Discounts

The biggest travel discounts originate with the airlines: They often have unused capacity, and they fill unsold seats by cutting prices.

They offer commissions up to 40 percent to consolidators, who buy or commit themselves to buy a specified portion of an airline's (or hotel's) yearly or seasonal capacity. Instead of the usual 8 to 10 percent, airlines offer override commissions of as much as 50 percent to high-volume consolidators. These overrides are supposed to be granted solely as sales incentives for travel agents; the official rules prohibit agents from passing any of this increase commission along to travelers. As a practical matter, however, consolidators rebate most of the override to retail agencies, which in turn sell the tickets.

This no-pretense discounting is against the law in some countries and contrary to airline industry rules everywhere, but it takes place anyhow. Every so often the various national regulatory agencies and the international and national airline industry associations clamp down briefly, but economic forces always bring discounting right back.

Indirect Rebates

Rather than offer a direct (cash-discount) rebate, airlines will often provide indirect rebates. An indirect rebate generally takes the form of some optional add-on travel service offered at a below-normal price when purchased in conjunction with an air ticket bought at list price. The add-on travel services usually consist of hotel accommodations or rental cars. Indirect rebates—or, if you prefer, airfare subsidies—avoid some of the stigma attached by the industry and government regulators to price cutting, but the net effect is the same if travelers can use the extra service provided at cut-rate prices.

Indirect rebates are offered for the same reasons as direct rebates. Quite often some airfares—even the lowest APEX fares—will turn out to be too high, in light of market conditions, to attract enough business. The most straightforward remedy is to reduce the fares to levels that will attract a satisfactory amount of business.

But straightforward remedies don't always appeal to the airlines or the governments that regulate them. Perhaps the United States and the European government involved can't agree on what a new fare level should be, or perhaps they're disagreeing about something entirely different. Airfares then serve as a surrogate battleground. Perhaps a foreign government wants to protect its major airline against competition from a low-fare airline and won't allow the low-fare airline to cut prices. For whatever combination of reasons, you frequently find situations in which airlines prefer to (or have to) subsidize relatively high fares rather than cut them.

Last year, many airlines offered reduced-rate hotel accommodations or rental cars as an add-on to the airfare. You may find comparable deals in spring, summer, and fall of 1988. The typical subsidy arrangement does not tie you down any more than the associated airfare. For example, if you find a free hotel or car rental for a week, it doesn't mean that you can stay in Europe only one week on that program. You're free to travel independently as far and as long as you wish, within the return limits of the basic ticket. If you want to keep the car or stay longer at the hotel, you pay for the extra time at regular rates. The land package is simply a way to add value to compensate for the high list price of the flight.

These subsidized airfare deals can be purchased directly from the airlines or through your travel agent. They're usually heavily and conspicuously promoted.

Generally, any subsidy introduced by a major line is quickly copied by its competitors. You very seldom see any one line with an obvious competitive edge. Low-fare airlines' subsidy programs, however, are sometimes ignored by the major lines, especially if the subsidy is obviously designed to compensate for the line's inability to offer as low a fare as it might wish. In any event, it might pay to shop around—sometimes one line will have a temporarily superior subsidy package during the specific time you want to travel.

Agency Discounts

Smaller discounts—no more than 10 percent and often 5 percent or less—originate with certain travel agents. Even when airlines and hotels don't offer large overrides or net wholesale prices, some agencies give their customers a discount by splitting the regular commission with them. This discount is usually offered in the form of a refund check, given to the customer at the time the ticket is purchased. In a few cases, the discount is in the form of credit for future travel purchases. These agencies often restrict their services to ticketing—their customers have to do their own research and make their own reservations.

Alternatively, a small but growing number of agencies charge a fixed fee rather than a percentage for their reservation and ticket-issuing services. Reservation and ticketing services are priced separately. Either way, you can expect to save no more than 10 percent with one of these agencies. Such a saving is better than none, but you can usually get a better deal somewhere else.

OUTLOOK FOR 1988

You can expect no shortage of discounts across the Atlantic this year. Last summer's prices are a good guide for what to expect:

- The lowest prices were on a number of the bigger charter programs. Whenever a charter program doesn't sell out well in advance, discount agencies typically sell seats at prices $50 to $100 below the advertised charter prices, which in turn are substantially below the lowest advertised promotional fares on the scheduled airlines.
- The lowest transatlantic scheduled-airline prices from New York were on Third World carriers such as Kuwait Airlines and Pakistan International. Several eastern-European airlines (including JAT) offered low prices to eastern Europe, the eastern part of western Europe, and the eastern Mediterranean. In most cases, the best buys were to cities other than the lines' home-base cities, reached by connecting flights. The reason was that whereas many foreign airlines offer discounts, they try to protect their home markets.
- Discount tickets on Canadian airlines were available from several major U.S. cities to Europe on connecting flights through Canadian gateway cities. These flights were several hours longer than nonstops from the main U.S. gateways; some required extensive layovers at a Canadian gateway, and you had to backtrack if you left from the East Coast.
- Some excellent discount fares to Europe were available on major U.S. and European airlines. To get the lowest rates, however, you often had to be flexible about schedules. On some lines you designated the dates you wanted to leave and return, but the airline chose the *specific* dates and flights and confirmed your final schedule a few days before departure.

CONVENIENCE

Discount and rebate travel can often be more convenient than cost-lier APEX excursion travel on the same or comparable airlines. Because of the type of distribution involved, these tickets tend to have less onerous advance-purchase and minimum-stay restrictions than the lowest list-price fares. On the other hand, the supplies can be limited, and the best deals sell out quickly.

Discount and rebate travel is also usually more convenient than charter travel. Service is on scheduled airlines, which offer daily or more frequent flights on most routes, compared with the weekly pattern more common for charters. Service quality can often be superior—many of the world's most highly esteemed airlines engage in these deals. On the other hand, airlines that push discount deals are at the low end of the quality spectrum.

Probably the biggest problem with discount transatlantic deals is that West Coast flights are often on airlines that offer only one- or two-stop service, rather than nonstop service. Thus, to save $50 to $150 (coupled with other below-APEX alternatives) you may have to spend as much as six hours extra travel time—a price that many travelers aren't willing to pay. Also, as is usually the case with special deals, discount tickets are often unavailable or very scarce during peak periods.

RISKS AND UNCERTAINTIES

These various discount tickets entail comparatively few inconveniences and risks. The major limitation is that they are almost always confined to the single airline that issued them. Itineraries that involve connecting flights require that all flights be on the same airline, or at least on two airlines with special fares established between them. Travelers cannot change airlines to enjoy better schedules or to alter itineraries. Similarly, refunds for unused tickets are, at best, available only through the issuing agent. In some cases, refunds can be difficult and time-consuming to obtain.

But discount tickets have some advantages, too. Unlike travelers on some charter programs, discount-ticket travelers know the identity of the airline they'll be flying before they buy. Also, these tickets avoid the problem of charter-tour operator failure. The passengers' tickets are their contracts with the airlines, and the airlines are responsible for fulfillment no matter what might happen to the retail or wholesale agent involved.

BUYING DISCOUNT TICKETS

Discount tickets obviously are not in the standard airline computer reservations systems that travel agents use. You can get them only from agencies that operate specifically in this marketplace.

A "bucket shop"—the term is appropriated from the securities industry—is the inelegant name given to a travel agency that sells airline tickets at true discount prices. But more and more full-service agencies are starting to handle discount airline tickets that used to be entirely the province of bucket shops. So if you have a regular travel agent, your first step should be to ask that agent if—and by how much—she or he can beat the list-price fares.

If you don't have a regular agent, or if your regular agent can't beat the official prices, you have to find a genuine bucket shop. Although no bucket shops are household names, such agencies do exist in most major cities. In the United States, the best way to locate them is to check major metropolitan newspapers. Bucket shops advertise themselves as low-fare specialists in small ads in weekend travel sections, and, in some cities, in classified travel or transportation sections.

Not all travel agents who advertise this way are bucket shops. Some agencies try to promote a low-fare image when all they can really claim is expertise in finding the best deal among the many scheduled-airline, list-price options. To save yourself time and money, you should first telephone agents that you think may be candidates and ask very specifically whether they can beat the list-price options you've found—whether they deal in discount, rebate, and bulk-fare tickets. Some may tell you they "can't discuss prices over the telephone," but you should make it clear that you'll be wasting their time as well as yours coming to their office if they can't beat the standard fares by a substantial margin.

Wherever situated, most bucket shops operate on a strictly cash basis—no credit cards, no personal checks. Tickets usually have to be prepaid. In this kind of business, you should protect yourself against possible shady operations. Avoid a final cash payment until the agent is ready to hand you your complete ticket.

LEGAL QUESTIONS

Discounting individual international airline tickets is currently against the law in the United States. Specifically, it is illegal for airlines and travel agents to rebate any part of the commission to a client, either directly or indirectly. The legal distinction between individual ticket discounting and bulk fares is that the latter are official airline tariffs, whereas individually discounted tickets, by definition, are not. Incidentally, these same types of discounting and rebating are perfectly legal for domestic travel.

The regulation applies only to airlines and agents. Travelers who buy discount tickets are not in violation of the law.

In practice, the distinction between legal and illegal discounts is almost invisible. Most discount and rebate deals can be structured as bulk-fare deals, or at least made to look enough like bulk-fare deals that virtually no one could tell the difference.

The U.S. government's enforcement policy on ticket discounting is ambiguous. The Department of Transportation insists that discounting should remain illegal but it admits that it has neither the resources nor the inclination to enforce the regulation. Enforcement actions are taken only—and only occasionally—when someone complains loudly enough to attract the department's notice. Even though the few enforcement actions taken over the last few years have not had a significant impact on the total discount market, the effect of enforcement has unfortunately been to confine ticket discounting to some of the smaller bucket shops and ethnic agencies, and probably to slow the growth of discounting.

Of course, many kinds of discounting break self-imposed airline-industry rules and regulations—which shouldn't worry travelers the least bit. The International Air Transport Association (IATA) keeps reminding its members of the evils of discounting; the members keep agreeing with IATA—while many keep on discounting.

Discounting may pose something of an ethical dilemma for some travelers. Even though you, as a traveler, are not breaking the law, you may be reluctant to buy the product of an illegal transaction between your suppliers. Clearly, many if not most below-list-price airfare deals are legal. But with some, you might be dealing with an agent or wholesaler who is breaking the law. It is almost impossible for you to ascertain whether any given deal is in full compliance with the law. If this concerns you, the best way to avoid a potential involvement in an illegal transaction is to ask the ticket supplier for some sort of written statement that the ticket is legally obtained. If the supplier is unable or unwilling to make such representation, and you consider it important, shop around for an alternative source.

There's another kind of legal problem, however, that can be a serious concern to travelers. Some discount airline tickets result from a complicated scheme in which residents of some Third World countries evade currency-conversion restrictions. A Nigerian, to use a frequent example, can pay a local travel agent in Nigerian currency (which can't be legally converted or taken out of the country). The agent then issues a miscellaneous charge order (MCO) denominated in hard currency at the official exchange rate. The MCO is mailed to a cooperating agency in a hard-currency country, where it can be exchanged at face value for an airline ticket. Of course, the MCO is heavily discounted in all these transactions, so the final selling agent sells the ticket to a traveler at a discount price. The Nigerian receives some hard currency from the agent—much less than the value of the local currency at the official exchange rate but bankable in Switzerland and beyond the reach of Nigerian officialdom. The ultimate loser in this scheme is the airline, which ends up owning blocked Nigerian currency.

The airlines are trying to stop currency-conversion discounting. They've become much more careful about issuing tickets against suspicious MCOs, and some airlines won't accept MCOs at all. Unfortunately, it's sometimes hard to identify such tickets. To protect yourself, avoid any ticket with "MCO" in the "issued in exchange for" box on the face of the ticket. And to prepare a possible legal recourse, ask the discounter for a written statement that the ticket was not obtained through a currency-conversion scam.

8

Quality Air Travel

Economy Class on major and low-fare airlines, charter flights, and bulk-fare deals are the most popular and least expensive ways to get to Europe. But what you get is bottom-of-the-line quality. With small (but important) differences, comfort and service range from barely adequate to terrible.

Genuine quality air services are available. Unfortunately, most of them are much more expensive—in some cases, ridiculously so. But some quality services are within the reach of economy-minded travelers, if you know where to find them.

BUSINESS CLASS

Business Class is the minimum level of transatlantic airline service that can genuinely be described as comfortable. Seating in 747s is no more crowded than eight seats across in a 2–2–2–2 pattern, and a few lines have only six seats across in a 2–2–2 arrangement. Some lines also have Business Class in the upper deck, with four seats across. In none will you find those detested middle seats. Pitch is at least 36 inches, more generous on some lines. You don't have to worry about comfort even if you're getting the last available seat.

Cabin services are also at a higher level. Drinks and movies are free in Business Class on all transatlantic airlines. Meal service is usually noticeably better, often with courses served separately on china rather than as a complete meal on a plastic tray.

The problem is, of course, that Business Class fares on most routes are more than double APEX or charter fares. In view of this tremendous price difference, Business Class really isn't an economically viable alternative for most vacationers. It's a much better buy for those travelers who *have* to pay full-fare Economy because they can't meet the restrictions on APEX and other cheaper services.

The only bargain in Business Class on a major airline is on El Al flights to Israel. You can upgrade to Business Class from any kind of Economy ticket—even APEX—for $97 each way from New York or $207 each way from Los Angeles. These inexpensive upgrades are available only on through flights; they are not available if you stop over in western Europe.

FIRST CLASS

These days, First Class service across the Atlantic is luxurious. All the lines that offer a First Class service use sleeper seats with folding leg rests (except on Alia's L-1011s). Seat rows are almost 5 feet apart. It's the only transatlantic service on which you can actually stretch out. Meal and drink services match the seating opulence.

Of course, the prices are high—three to six times the cost of APEX or a charter. Clearly, First Class caters to people who can spend a lot of money for top-quality travel.

Nevertheless, if you want to enjoy the best the airlines have to offer, there are ways to enjoy First Class service without paying the full tab. As noted in chapter 6, you can sometimes buy a companion First Class trip for about the same cost as an APEX or charter ticket. Also, as described in chapter 9, you can save up to 70 percent by buying frequent-flier coupons for First Class travel from other individuals or from a coupon broker.

FIRST-CLASS CHARTER

When a charter program uses airplanes normally used for scheduled service, chances are there will be First Class and/or Business

Class sections on that airplane. When this is the case, most charter operators offer the high-quality seating as a premium-price option. In 1987, First Class charter costs were usually $100 to $700 higher than the regular charter price, but there's no standard range among charter offerings. The premium is set at whatever level the operator thinks will yield maximum revenues.

In a few cases, the operator features full First Class service in addition to the seating—unlimited free drinks and the airline's normal First Class meal service. In most cases, however, only the seating is different, and everyone gets the same bar service and meals. Again, it depends on the operator.

The First Class charter is almost always the least expensive way to enjoy a high-quality trip. Although the premium charged represents a substantial percentage increase over the usual charter price, the cost is still much lower than regular First Class service on a scheduled airline.

For example, one Balair program last summer used Swissair DC-10s for nonstop charters from San Francisco and Miami to Zurich. Travelers who rode in the Business Class seats paid a premium of about $250 round-trip (it varied slightly by city of departure), while travelers who wanted the full sleeper First Class seats paid about $700 more. This is less than one-third the usual First Class fare. On this program, only the seating was different—all passengers received the same cabin service.

Of course, compared with ordinary charters, only the cost and comfort (and possibly the cabin service) are different on First and Business Class charters. The convenience and contingency factors are the same.

PREMIUM SERVICE ON LOW-FARE AIRLINES

Highland Express, Icelandair, Tower, and Virgin Atlantic all offer premium service:

- Business Class on Highland Express provides sleeper seats comparable with First Class on major airlines.
- Icelandair's Saga Class provides more legroom than standard Economy but uses the same narrow six-across seating.
- Tower has a few First Class seats similar to Business Class on major airlines.

- Virgin Atlantic offers an Upper Class option with sleeper
  seats, comparable to major airlines' First Class. Upper Class
  service also includes complimentary helicopter or limousine
  service in both New York and London.

These fares are far below either First or even Business Class fares
on the major lines. Accordingly, they represent a good value for
travelers who want high-quality service. As in the case of high-
quality charter services, however, only the quality is different—
convenience and contingency factors are independent of in-flight
comfort or class of service.

9

Other Possibilities

In case promotional fares, low-fare airlines, charters, bulk fares, last-minute deals, and discount tickets don't give you enough options, there are other ways you can keep your transatlantic air-travel costs down.

FREQUENT-TRAVELER COUPONS

Frequent-traveler awards were first mentioned in chapter 6 in connection with "companion" tickets. Most of the awards in these programs, however, consist of upgrades (from Economy to Business or First Class) and "free" trips within various regions. Many provide for trips from the United States to Europe; coupons are available on both U.S. and foreign airlines.

These programs are all quite similar. An individual enrolls with an airline—some programs require a modest entry fee; others do not. Then the traveler's mileage for each flight taken is logged by the airline and totaled. On some lines, awards can be earned with as little as 5,000 accumulated miles; on others, the minimum awards require as much as 20,000 miles. Obviously, the higher the mileage, the greater the value of the award.

Again, the prevailing terminology can cause confusion. These mileage-based, frequent-traveler benefits are properly termed "awards." But since the earliest free-trip awards offered in airline promotional programs were issued in the form of coupons, the term *coupon* has become the accepted but unofficial expression for any sort of travel benefit that can be bought and sold after it has been issued.

Although most members of frequent-flier programs use their mileage credits themselves for free travel or upgrades, some prefer to convert their benefits into cash. These frequent fliers supply the inventory for the coupon marketplace. The coupons, however, are not so easily sold—or bought. All airlines require that each coupon for a frequent-flier benefit be issued in the name of the traveler who will use it. Once issued, the coupon is not transferable. A seller cannot ask an airline to issue a coupon until he or she can specify the name of the traveler who will use it. Accordingly, the coupon market involves three steps:

1. A frequent flier with accumulated mileage credit (the seller) offers mileage accruals to a coupon broker. The broker pays the seller for the mileage and adds the benefit to the inventory the broker has for sale.
2. When a buyer agrees to purchase a coupon from the broker, the broker provides the buyer's name to the seller of the frequent-flier benefit. The seller then asks the airline to issue the specified benefit in that buyer's name. When the seller receives the coupon, he or she forwards it to the broker, who sends it to the buyer.
3. Using the coupon, the buyer makes reservations and has a ticket issued, either directly by the airline or through a travel agent. The buyer travels under her or his own name.

Since this entire program often takes up to a month, you have to arrange for your coupon well in advance (brokers can arrange express issuance and delivery from some airlines, at your expense). But once you have your coupon, your plans can be flexible. After issue, a coupon giving you a wide range of destinations is usually good for a full year and the ticket you buy with it is also good for a year. Coupon-based tickets typically do not require an advance-purchase period, and reservations can be shifted right up to the last minute. Regular coupon users often keep one on hand, ready for use at any time.

The coupon market peaked in 1986. Last year, most airlines tightened transfer rules in an attempt to curtail the coupon market. As a result, prices have gone up and options are fewer. But coupons can still be an attractive option.

The main drawback to these coupons, for economy-minded travelers, is that the best deals are for First Class and Business Class travel, not for Economy Class. In a buy-and-sell market, the per-mile value of First Class awards is two to three times the value of the Economy Class awards. Coupon dealers obviously ask people who are planning to sell their mileage benefits to accumulate miles toward First Class awards, and tend to concentrate on business at the higher end of the market.

It's hard to find any coupon deals through brokers that are less expensive than APEX to Europe. By contrast, First Class round-trip ticket *coupons* on major airlines from any domestic point to any offered point in Europe or the Middle East were available for about $2,000 to $2,500 in mid-1987. These coupons provide for travel that would cost, for example, up to $6,000 at *regular* fares for round-trip travel from the West Coast to eastern Mediterranean cities. Coupons are clearly an extremely good way to save money if you demand the best quality air travel has to offer.

Because coupons typically apply to travel from any U.S. point on an issuing airline's system to various points in Europe, savings are obviously greatest for relatively long trips, especially from the West Coast. Also, coupons must save money for travelers who can't abide by APEX advance-purchase and minimum/maximum-stay restrictions—but here, the utility may be limited by the time required to obtain the necessary coupons. The best use of coupons is for high-quality travel at relatively low cost. Savings can easily amount to thousands of dollars per trip.

Buying and selling coupons may not be in violation of any law. But the major lines state that transfer by sale or barter, directly or through brokers, is against their rules. Some limit transfers to relatives of program members, but these airlines define family broadly to grandparents, cousins, and in-laws, permitting transfers to travelers with different surnames and giving brokers the leeway they need to circumvent the rules. As might be expected, the airlines and brokers take very different positions:

- The airlines state that it is against their rules for frequent-flier members to sell benefits or for other travelers to buy them, that these rules are "vigorously" enforced, and that travelers detected trying to use tickets obtained with purchased coupons are denied boarding and have their tickets confiscated. The airlines warn potential users that they risk having to pay full-fare Coach or Economy Class for alternative transportation if they are caught trying to use a ticket obtained through a purchased coupon.

· The brokers respond that of the thousands of travelers to whom they have sold coupons, only about a dozen or so have been denied boarding by an airline. In such cases, most brokers claim they either issue another coupon on a different airline or cover the cost of alternate transportation so that the traveler does not incur out-of-pocket expenses. They also say that several of the travelers who had been denied boarding had openly boasted of their coupon purchase within hearing of airline boarding agents, in effect inviting airline action.

If you want to purchase coupons, you don't necessarily have to deal with a broker. If you know a frequent flier with excess-mileage benefits, you can make an arrangement directly and probably save quite a bit. But these private transactions are subject to the same limitations as transactions through brokers.

How else can you locate a coupon deal? Individual coupon sellers normally advertise in the classified sections of major metropolitan daily newspapers, under the same headings as discount-ticket sources. They also advertise in the classified section of the *Wall Street Journal*, under "Miscellaneous."

But most coupon travelers will probably wind up buying from one of the coupon brokers that have come into being in response to the burgeoning frequent-traveler programs. Although the coupon market can be quite dynamic, it appears that at any given time prices tend to be uniform. Presumably, the various brokers keep themselves aware of other dealers' buy and sell prices and make sure that they remain competitive.

Brokers, like individual sellers, advertise in classifieds and travel sections. Recent editions of the *Wall Street Journal* and *The New York Times* carried several ads from coupon brokers interested in buying and selling. A few coupon brokers also have small display ads in business travel magazines and in *Travel Weekly*, the travel-industry tabloid.

The following coupon brokers were active in mid-1987: Airline

Coupon Co., 800-354-4489 (800-338-0099 in CA); American Coupon Exchange, 800-222-9699 (800-222-9599 in CA); Coupon Bank, 800-292-9250 (800-331-1076 in CA); Coupon Broker, 800-247-2891 (303-759-1953 in CO); Coupon Connection, 800-552-0700 (602-829-7300 in AZ); Flyer's Edge, 312-256-8200; Go in Class, 800-872-8587 (312-236-9696 in IL); Horizon Group, 800-436-9377 (213-471-1160 in CA); International Air Coupon Exchange, 800-558-0053 (713-781-1543 in TX); Travel Deluxe International, 212-826-6644.

OTHER COUPONS

Transatlantic airlines get involved in other coupon promotions from time to time. In 1986, for example, TWA sold upgrade discount tickets through catalogs of mail-order companies. In mid-1987, the Travel Channel Club offered coupons as a membership premium, valid for a 25-percent discount on TWA.

Over the last few years, TWA has been involved in more transatlantic coupon promotions than any other major airline. But you never know which one will try something else. Regardless of the line, however, remember some typical limitations that may not be prominently mentioned in the promotional materials:

- Most ticket discounts are blacked out during the most popular travel seasons. Blackout periods typically include the peak summer season, the Christmas–New Year period, the Easter–spring vacation periods, and even the major holiday weekends.
- Many apply only to Economy Class service, not to Business or First Class.
- Some may provide discounts only on full-fare Economy tickets, not on such less expensive promotional fares as APEX. For most travelers, such promotions are a sham—in past promotions of this type, the discounted fares have often been higher than undiscounted APEX fares.

FOREIGN-CURRENCY PURCHASE

International air fares are adjusted only infrequently to compensate for shifts in exchange rates among various major currencies. Also, some fares are established in both Europe and the United

States with reference to market "price points" rather than exact exchange-rate parity—that is, at specific price levels that marketers deem "sellable" for a big-ticket purchase. The net result of these factors was that throughout 1987, airline tickets purchased in European currency were often less expensive than tickets for comparable trips purchased with U.S. dollars.

Foreign-currency purchase represented a fantastic value in late 1984 and early 1985, when the dollar was at an all-time high value compared with most European currencies. At that time some tickets bought in European currencies cost about half of what comparable tickets cost in U.S. dollars. By 1987, however, the dollar had dropped substantially against most European currencies, and the foreign-currency advantage had largely disappeared.

Keep this option in mind whenever the dollar is strong. But remember the basic limitation: Tickets have to be priced in the currency of the country in which the trip originates. Thus, you cannot buy a pound-priced New York–London–New York ticket in New York—and you can't even have a friend buy one for you in London and send it to you. You cannot buy a round-the-world ticket in pounds and start your trip in the United States. If the trip starts in the United States, the ticket has to be sold at the dollar price.

Most of the best major-airline promotional fares are based on round-trip ticket purchase. Prices are usually much lower than two of the cheapest one-way fares—so much so that you're better off with a dollar-priced promotional fare, even though you may have to pay more for it than a European resident who buys the same kind of ticket to visit the United States. But you can sometimes use the exchange rates to save on inexpensive one-way fares such as Standby, or on Business or First Class.

You do not have to buy foreign-currency tickets in Europe. As long as you're buying tickets for a trip that originates in Europe (as far as that ticket is concerned), you can buy it in the United States. Your price is simply the quoted foreign-currency price converted to dollars on the day you buy. Any airline office or travel agent can handle the deal. Note that there is nothing illegal about this kind of foreign-currency purchase, nor is it against airline rules. As long as the currency in which you buy is convertible, there's no problem. This kind of purchase is completely different from buying tickets issued against *blocked* currency (see page 73).

Of course, the attractiveness of purchasing tickets in European currencies depends on the exchange rates at the time you're buying. It's clear, however, that any time you're using an option for which a round-trip costs the same as two one-way tickets—Standby, low-fare airline, or full-fare Economy, Business, or First Class—you should definitely find out what the return trip would cost in European currency as well as in dollars. The airlines will tell you the European fares. Then, get the current exchange rates and calculate the dollar cost of your return ticket in Europe. If it's below the official dollar price, buy your return ticket at foreign-currency prices.

10

Stopovers and Connections

Travelers to Europe who live in big East Coast cities don't have to worry as much about en route stopovers and connection headaches as people who live in the U.S. interior or on the West Coast. But for those travelers who do not live in the Northeast, stopovers and connections can be important considerations.

THE STOPOVER HEADACHE

Many of the most troublesome kinds of traveler quandaries involve stopovers. Quite a few travelers bound for Europe from interior or western U.S. cities would like to stop over in New York, Boston, Washington, Chicago, or Miami on their trip, either going or coming back, for business or personal reasons. But the best major airline promotional fares on most routes generally do not allow any en route stopovers. The cheapest through fares that officially permit stopovers are full-fare Economy, which are almost always much more expensive than the low-cost alternatives.

A few transatlantic routes do allow East Coast gateway stopovers with APEX fares; see details in chapter 11. Unfortunately, the routes on which stopovers are permitted are usually those to the less popular European gateways. The stopover privileges are, in effect, bonuses designed to make the gateways more competitive. Also, some travelers would like stopovers in westernmost European cities on their way to or from some internal point, for example, a London or Madrid stopover on a trip to Zurich or Rome. You could buy a promotional-fare ticket to the western gateway and an internal European flight to get to and from the internal point. The catch to this approach is the high internal European airfares. The cheapest internal European round-trip flight of this kind is likely to cost more than your round-trip across the Atlantic. What can you do? Employ the following strategies:

1. If you're visiting the eastern Mediterranean—Athens, Belgrade, Cairo, Tel Aviv—the APEX fares do allow limited European stopovers, either free or at nominal extra cost.
2. If one of the cities you want to visit happens to have a good market in discount tickets (London and Amsterdam have been the best bets in previous years), you can base your trip on a cheaply priced round-trip ticket to one of these cities, then go to a bucket shop and purchase a separate round-trip ticket to your final destination city. This approach can be risky and time-consuming, since it will take some time for you to find and deal with a bucket shop in Europe, a good bucket-shop flight might not be available when you want to travel, and changes in local markets might dry up the supply of cheap flights when you're looking for one. This approach should be a last resort.
3. For domestic stopovers, you can sometimes buy two separate promotional-fare tickets—one from your originating city to an East Coast gateway, the other from the East Coast gateway to Europe. Schedule flights to allow you the desired stopover.

Aside from these limited opportunities, most travelers resist the generally high cost of internal European flying and arrange stopovers in Europe by car or train, or explore open-jaw APEX fares and take a train between the two cities. If your domestic ticket is issued separately from your international ticket, check the restrictions on both tickets carefully. A delayed flight could make your connecting ticket worthless.

SCHEDULES AND CONNECTIONS

Enough large European cities will have nonstop or direct flights to satisfy many travelers who live in the largest U.S. cities. But many people who live outside the top few U.S. metropolitan areas will undoubtedly have to make at least one connection. If you have to do so, you'll lower the irritation level substantially if you can avoid connections through Kennedy Airport (New York). Atlanta, Boston, Charlotte, Dallas, Denver, Miami, Newark, Washington, and even O'Hare (Chicago) are usually better alternatives. However, to many European cities, Kennedy is your only choice.

Kennedy does, however, provide one unique schedule advantage: British Airways and Pan American offer daytime nonstops from Kennedy to London. Some people will welcome such flights as an alternative to the overnight flights that are the only option for all other eastbound transatlantic flights. If you hate overnight flying, this option is attractive.

In general, for reasons of maximum aircraft-use efficiency, the combination of elapsed flight times and differences in European and North American time zones confines the departure and arrival times of flights between the United States and Europe to a very small window. The only time you have any real schedule options is when you start from the West Coast. On routes without nonstop service, you can either (1) fly nonstop to a major European gateway, then take a connecting European flight, or (2) fly to New York or Chicago and connect with a nonstop to your destination. The fares are usually the same; base your choice on convenience.

Many travelers may prefer the *first* option, especially if the local European connection is relatively short, because:

1. Total flight times can be several hours shorter—the nonstop polar-route flights from the West Coast to Europe are hundreds of miles shorter than connecting routes through New York or Chicago.
2. By splitting your eastbound flight into one long segment (nine to twelve hours, West Coast to Europe) and a short add-on, you allow more time to relax (maybe even to sleep) on the overnight segment. The alternative New York connection involves shorter overnight transatlantic flights;

when you figure the time required for takeoff and ascent, dinner, and (possibly) a movie, you have almost no time left to get any rest. Westbound, this factor isn't as important.

3. But with this option, you'll probably leave in the afternoon and arrive at your final destination the next evening—perhaps later than you'd like.

The second option has some advantages. If your connection in Europe would require a long European flight (for example, London to Athens), you might well be better off connecting through New York. The Economy Class service-quality standards on most intra-European flights are poor. With this option, you typically leave the West Coast early in the morning and arrive at your final destination the next morning or early afternoon.

11

The Outlook for Airfares—1988

The following listing presents a summary of peak-season 1988 transatlantic airfares to 25 major gateways in Europe and the eastern Mediterranean. Our emphasis is on the least expensive major-airline fare available in each market. Other major-airline fare levels are also listed, along with some comments and predictions about low-fare airline, charter, and bulk-fare opportunities.

Fares are quoted for four U.S.-origin areas. Chicago and New York are obvious departure points. Texas refers to either Dallas or Houston, depending on which city has the most direct service on each route, and West Coast refers to either Los Angeles or San Francisco, on the same basis.

To facilitate comparison, all fares are shown as round-trips—including fares that are also available one way. One-way fares for full-fare Economy, Business, and First Class are usually half the round-trip cost.

Fares quoted apply to the most direct (preferably nonstop) services available. Some airlines occasionally offer lower fares on flights that require connections, especially on Business and First Class. These fares are not listed, but you should ask your travel agent about them if you don't mind an extra stop or connection. However, you aren't apt to find any such reductions on the lowest APEX fares.

The intent of this comparison is to illustrate both the substantial differences between the various classes of fares and the different seasonal patterns that prevail to different destinations. But this book should not be your definitive reference for complete or up-to-date fares on any one route. As an indication of the complexity in airfares, consider that the computer printouts used to construct this simplified list often show 30 to 40 different fares for each route. Make sure that your travel agent, the airline ticket office, or anyone else making your reservations checks to ensure that you are receiving the lowest possible fare within your requirements.

In general, the season in which your trip originates determines the seasonal fare to be paid. However, if your itinerary includes, for example, a weekend flight going over but a midweek flight coming back, your fare will usually be one-half of the sum of the two different round-trip fares. Open-jaw trips (see page 11) are figured the same way: the fare is one-half of the round-trip fare between the points.

ALTERNATIVE GATEWAYS

Your itinerary will generally establish the gateway city or cities in Europe to and from which you'll fly. Your attention should therefore be directed to finding the best alternative for those specific destinations.

As a rule of thumb, you'll probably pay $500 to $1,000 minimum for your air travel, plus about $500 for local travel within Europe. Depending on your standards, your daily hotel and meal costs will be anywhere from $50 to $200 per person. So on a three-week trip your average per-person, out-of-pocket cost for just being in Europe will be between $125 and $265 a day. Clearly, then, you would have to save at least double that amount per ticket before you could justify flying to an alternative gateway that required an extra day of ground travel to get to or from the places you really wanted to visit.

In rare cases, however, it will be to your advantage to use a different gateway city, in a different country, just to save on air travel—prevailing high fares to one city may make a flight to a less expensive gateway an attractive option. You should give careful consideration to this approach in cases where you're looking for fares substantially lower than major-airline APEX fares, but you can't find any low-fare airline service, charters, bulk-fare deals, or discounts to your preferred destination.

If, however, you are planning a tour of several countries, you might be relatively indifferent about which gateways to use. Your range of options, then, will be broadened—you can let relative airfare levels (as well as car-rental costs, if you're driving) help determine the route you take. In this connection, note in chapter 14 that Belgium, Germany, Luxembourg, and the Netherlands offer attractive combinations of low airfare options and low rental-car costs compared with adjacent countries. If your plans already include one of these countries, they look like especially attractive gateways this year.

In any case, the only way to get an idea of what you can expect to spend is to tabulate your options on a country-by-country basis.

For 1988, all APEX fares carry a cancellation fee of $75 to $100 or a percentage of the fare. There is now a $13-per-ticket fee (customs user and federal inspection fees and international air-transportation tax) added to the cost of the ticket at the time of purchase. In 1987 some carriers were charging fuel surcharges of $8 each way.

Amsterdam

Major Airlines

| | Round-trip fare to Amsterdam from | | | |
Fare Basis	New York	Chicago	Texas	West Coast
Cheapest excursion	$ 738	$ 808	$ 703	$ 921
Full fare				
Economy	1,442	1,570	1,606	1,782
Business Class	1,676	1,874	1,878	2,328
First Class	3,212	3,606	3,606	4,162

Restrictions on Lowest Available Fare
Peak season: June 1–September 14
Advance purchase: 21 days
Minimum stay: 1 day
Weekend supplement: $50 each way
Stopovers: none
Children's fare: 67%
Cancellation penalty: $75

Low-Fare Airlines

Although there is no direct, low-fare airline service to Amsterdam, a traveler may take Virgin Atlantic to London and use their $55 fare to Maastricht, Holland (about an hour's driving time from Amsterdam).

Charter and Bulk Fare

Amsterdam has always been a major charter destination, so look for some large programs. A Dutch charter specialist, Martinair, operated nonstop or direct charters from many U.S. cities in 1987 and will probably repeat this year. Peak summer fares should be about $400 to $450 from New York, around $500 to $550 from Chicago, and around $625 to $700 from the West Coast.

Athens

Major Airlines

	Round-trip fare to Athens from			
Fare Basis	New York	Chicago	Texas	West Coast
Cheapest excursion	$ 997	$ 940	—	—
Full fare				
Economy	1,818	1,158	1,176	1,231
Business Class	2,500	2,967	2,830	3,433
First Class	4,400	5,073	5,080	5,785

Restrictions on Lowest Available Fare

Peak season: June 1–August 31
Advance purchase: 14 days
Minimum stay: 7 days
Weekend supplement: none
Stopovers: none
Children's fare: 75%
Cancellation penalty: $75

Low-Fare Airlines

There has been no low-fare airline service direct to Athens in the past, and none is likely for 1988. You can use Icelandair in conjunction with Luxair (via Luxembourg) and get better fares than offered on direct flights.

Charter and Bulk Fare

Charter volume has been heavy in recent years. You can expect the same for 1988. Summer fares from New York should range from $550 to $650, with one ways available from around $350 to $400. Most of the action is from New York; don't expect much from the interior cities or the West Coast. There was bulk-fare service at about the same prices as charters in 1987.

Belgrade

Major Airlines

	Round-trip fare to Belgrade from			
Fare Basis	New York	Chicago	Texas	West Coast
Cheapest excursion	$ 900	$1,000	—	$1,083
Full fare				
Economy	1,646	1,812	—	1,986
Business Class	1,844	2,010	—	2,754
First Class	3,386	3,590	—	—

Restrictions on Lowest Available Fare

Peak season: June 1–August 14
Advance purchase: 21 days
Minimum stay: 14 days
Weekend supplement: $50 each way
Stopovers: none
Children's fare: 67%
Cancellation penalty: $75

Low-Fare Airlines

No low-fare airlines serve Yugoslavia, and this is unlikely to change in 1988.

Charter and Bulk Fare

Nothing dramatic is expected. Yugoslavia is a fairly minor destination for Americans, and is generally isolated from some of the more competitive market forces.

Brussels

Major Airlines

Fare Basis	Round-trip fare to Brussels from			
	New York	Chicago	Texas	West Coast
Cheapest excursion	$ 698	$ 778	—	$ 881
Full fare				
Economy	1,447	1,668	—	2,102
Business Class	1,676	1,874	—	2,328
First Class	3,212	3,606	—	4,162

Restrictions on Lowest Available Fare
Peak season: June 1–September 14
Advance purchase: 7 days
Minimum stay: 4 days
Weekend supplement: none
Stopovers: one at each U.S. gateway; extra cost: none
Children's fare: 67%
Cancellation penalty: $75
Other special conditions: $75 for one change

Low-Fare Airlines
There is no low-fare airline serving Brussels from the United States.

Charter and Bulk Fare
Most of the low-fare service to Brussels seems to be through bulk-fare deals rather than charters. Bulk-fare deals were offered in 1987 at around $550 from New York and $775 from the West Coast. A few charter programs will also be offered in 1988.

Cairo

Major Airlines

Fare Basis	Round-trip fare to Cairo from			
	New York	Chicago	Texas	West Coast
Cheapest excursion	$ 999	$1,109	$1,127	$1,112
Full fare				
Economy	2,076	2,204	2,022	2,984
Business Class	2,284	2,722	2,486	3,194
First Class	3,382	4,482	4,512	5,194

Restrictions on Lowest Available Fare
Peak season: May 15–September 14
Advance purchase: 14 days
Minimum stay: 6–7 days
Weekend supplement: none
Stopovers: one in either Rome or Athens; others: $75 each
Children's fare: 67%
Cancellation penalty: $75

Low-Fare Airlines
There is no low-fare airline serving Cairo from the United States.

Charter and Bulk Fare
Don't expect any charters to Cairo this summer, though you may
see some bulk-fare tickets for $650 to $700 from New York, $850
from Chicago, and $900 from the West Coast.

Copenhagen

Major Airlines

| | Round-trip fare to Copenhagen from | | | |
Fare Basis	New York	Chicago	Texas	West Coast
Cheapest excursion	$ 875	$ 985	$1,003	$1,085
Full fare				
Economy	1,556	1,770	2,224	2,304
Business Class	1,556	1,770	2,224	2,304
First Class	3,582	3,628	4,450	4,166

Restrictions on Lowest Available Fare
Peak season: June 1–August 14
Advance purchase: 21 days
Minimum stay: 10 days
Weekend supplement: $50 each way
Stopovers: none
Children's fare: 67%
Cancellation penalty: $75
Other special conditions: Ticketing required at the time of reserva-
tion

　　Comment: Look for fares to Scandinavia to remain higher than fares to other European destinations for comparable distances. All passengers who pay full-fare Economy are entitled to Business Class.

Low-Fare Airlines
Tower Air is operating flights from New York once a week. Flights are nonstop.

Charter and Bulk Fare
Scandinavia has permitted only a trickle of charter service from the United States in the past. You probably won't see much this year either. Bulk fares on the Tower Air flights were $478 in 1987.

Dublin

Major Airlines

	Round-trip fare to Dublin from			
Fare Basis	New York	Chicago	Texas	West Coast
Cheapest excursion	$ 629	$ 729	$ 757	$ 812
Full fare				
Economy	—	—	1,332	1,508
Business Class	1,510	1,884	1,898	2,478
First Class	2,840	2,812	4,146	—

Restrictions on Lowest Available Fare
Peak season: June 1–September 14
Advance purchase: 21 days
Minimum stay: 7 days
Weekend supplement: $25 each way (except New York)
Stopovers: at U.S. gateway
Children's fare: 67%
Cancellation penalty: $75
Other special conditions: $100 for one change

Low-Fare Airlines
No direct or nonstop low-fare airline service to Ireland is expected. If you want to use a low-fare airline, your best bet is to take Virgin Atlantic to London and then either fly directly, take the train-ferry, or take a fly-drive package.

Charter and Bulk Fare

Ireland has enjoyed good charter service over the years, but most flights serve Shannon.

Frankfurt

Major Airlines

Fare Basis	Round-trip fare to Frankfurt from			
	New York	Chicago	Texas	West Coast
Cheapest excursion	$ 756	$ 823	$ 713	$ 917
Full fare				
Economy	1,556	1,730	1,766	1,914
Business Class	1,724	2,088	1,926	2,338
First Class	3,212	3,606	3,606	4,162

Restrictions on Lowest Available Fare

Peak season: June 1–September 14
Advance purchase: 21 days
Minimum stay: 7 days
Weekend supplement: approximately $50
Stopovers: none
Children's fare: 67%
Cancellation penalty: $75

Low-Fare Airlines

No low-fare airline flies to Germany. Virgin Atlantic offers a $25 add-on fare from London to Maastricht, Holland (about an hour's driving time from Germany). Icelandair's through fares in conjunction with Luxair are lower than fares on direct flights.

Charter and Bulk Fare

Germany is an extremely active charter and bulk-fare destination, with big programs on its two charter airlines, Condor and LTU, as well as on U.S. carriers. Charter programs were run from more than a dozen U.S. cities in 1987, and the pattern should continue for 1988. Peak summer round-trip fares should be $475 to $550 from New York, $550 to $650 from Chicago, $600 to $700 from Texas, and $700 to $850 from the West Coast. Bulk fares at about the same levels were offered in 1987.

Geneva
Major Airlines

Fare Basis	Round-trip fare to Geneva from			
	New York	Chicago	Texas	West Coast
Cheapest excursion	$ 776	$ 844	$ 904	$ 959
Full fare				
Economy	1,506	1,694	—	—
Business Class	1,694	1,916	1,896	2,604
First Class	3,228	3,614	3,980	4,590

Restrictions on Lowest Available Fare
Peak season: June 1–September 14
Advance purchase: 21 days
Minimum stay: 7 days
Weekend supplement: $100 round-trip ($50 each way)
Stopovers: none
Children's fare: 67%
Cancellation penalty: $75

Low-Fare Airlines
No low-fare airline flies to Geneva.

Charter and Bulk Fare
Several operators offered low-cost charters to Switzerland in 1987, serving both Geneva and Zurich. Peak-season round-trip fares should be about $500 to $600 from New York, $650 from Chicago and Texas, and $800 to $900 from the West Coast. Bulk fares at about the same levels were available in 1987.

Helsinki
Major Airlines

Fare Basis	Round-trip fare to Helsinki from			
	New York	Chicago	Texas	West Coast
Cheapest excursion	$ 996	$1,095	$1,316	$1,768
Full fare				
Economy	1,548	1,990	—	2,088
Business Class	1,862	1,992	2,192	2,484
First Class	3,038	3,768	4,624	3,868

Restrictions on Lowest Available Fare
Peak season: June 1–August 14
Advance purchase: 21 days
Minimum stay: 7 days
Weekend supplement: yes
Stopovers: none
Children's fare: 67%
Cancellation penalty: $75

Low-Fare Airlines
There was no activity in 1987, and none is expected in 1988.

Charter and Bulk Fare
Scandinavia has permitted only a trickle of charter service from the United States. Bulk fares in 1987 were about $700 from New York, $925 from Texas, and $975 from the West Coast.

Lisbon

Major Airlines

| | Round-trip fare to Lisbon from | | | |
Fare Basis	New York	Chicago	Texas	West Coast
Cheapest excursion	$ 447	$ 577	$ 595	$ 650
Full fare				
Economy	1,292	1,496	1,496	1,656
Business Class	1,976	2,420	2,306	2,886
First Class	3,598	4,248	4,446	4,960

Restrictions on Lowest Available Fare
Peak season: June 16–August 15
Advance purchase: 14 days
Minimum stay: 7 days
Weekend supplement: $50–$70 round-trip
Stopovers: none
Children's fare: 67%
Cancellation penalty: $75

Low-Fare Airlines
None.

Charter and Bulk Fare

Several charter programs operate to Portugal each year, especially from U.S. cities with strong ethnic ties—in particular, Boston and New York. Look for round-trip fares at about the same level as last year, around $500 to $600 from the East Coast.

London

Major Airlines

| | Round-trip fare to London from | | | |
Fare Basis	New York	Chicago	Texas	West Coast
Cheapest excursion	$ 688	$ 689	$ 689	$ 815
Full fare				
Economy	1,462	1,096	2,176	1,340
Business Class	2,212	3,078	3,284	3,346
First Class	4,342	5,086	5,210	5,382
Concorde	5,712	—	—	—

Restrictions on Lowest Available Fare

Peak season: June 1–September 30
Advance purchase: 21 days
Minimum stay: 7 days
Weekend supplement: $50–$70 each way
Stopovers: none
Children's fare: 67%
Cancellation penalty: $50
Other special conditions: $50 for one change

Low-Fare Airlines

London continues to be an active low-fare airline market.

Charter and Bulk Fare

London has been an active charter market for some years, with service from about a dozen U.S. cities. Bulk-fare seats are widely offered. Look for charters and bulk fares at peak-season, round-trip rates of $400 to $500 from New York, $550 to $650 from Chicago, and $600 to $750 from the West Coast.

Luxembourg

Major Airlines

| Fare Basis | Round-trip fare to Luxembourg from | | | |
	New York	Chicago	Texas	West Coast
Cheapest excursion	$ 599	$ 689	$ 866	$ 921
Full fare				
Economy	679	796	1,606	—
Business Class	779	869	—	—
First Class	—	—	—	—

Restrictions on Lowest Available Fare
Peak season: June 1–September 7
Advance purchase: 14–21 days
Minimum stay: 7 days
Stopovers: free in Ireland
Children's fare: 67%

Comments: Icelandair will probably retain its special place in transatlantic travel with its competitive fares to Luxembourg. U.S. gateways—Baltimore, Detroit, and Orlando—offer passengers the option of not having to connect through New York. Icelandair's new Saga (Business) Class provides extra legroom (35-inch pitch) but retains 3–3 across seating.

Icelandair may be particularly attractive to travelers who can't conform to the usual advance-purchase requirements or minimum/maximum-stay requirements of APEX fares. The airline also offers easy connections to numerous destinations within Europe. Icelandair provides free bus service from Luxembourg to Germany, Belgium, and Holland. In addition, the airline offers passengers a special rail fare to Paris, or to any city in Switzerland on Swiss Federal Railways. For passengers destined for Stockholm, Bergen, Göteborg, Oslo, and Copenhagen, there is a free 24-hour stopover for one-way flights and a 48-hour stopover for round-trips in Reykjavik, Iceland.

Low-Fare Airlines
Icelandair is the continent's only low-fare airline.

Charter and Bulk Fare
Icelandair preempts all the action here.

Madrid
Major Airlines

| Fare Basis | Round-trip fare to Madrid from | | | |
	New York	Chicago	Texas	West Coast
Cheapest excursion	$ 652	$ 762	$ 780	$ 835
Full fare				
Economy	1,298	1,426	1,462	1,638
Business Class	2,150	2,594	2,480	3,060
First Class	3,600	4,250	4,280	4,962

Restrictions on Lowest Available Fare
Peak season: June 1–August 15
Advance purchase: 14 days
Minimum stay: 7 days
Weekend supplement: $70 round-trip
Stopovers: none
Children's fare: 67%
Cancellation penalty: $75

Low-Fare Airlines
None.

Charter and Bulk Fare
Several charter programs operate to Spain each year. Charter and bulk fares will probably range from $450 to $550 from the East Coast and $650 to $750 from the West Coast.

Milan
Major Airlines

| Fare Basis | Round-trip fare to Milan from | | | |
	New York	Chicago	Texas	West Coast
Cheapest excursion	$ 849	$ 949	$ 977	$1,032
Full fare				
Economy	1,468	1,668	1,632	1,830
Business Class	2,108	2,408	2,310	2,892
First Class	3,906	4,536	4,586	5,082

Restrictions on Lowest Available Fare
Peak season: June 1–September 14
Advance purchase: 21 days
Minimum stay: 7 days
Weekend supplement: yes
Stopovers: none; open-jaw permitted
Children's fare: 67%
Cancellation penalty: $75

Low-Fare Airlines
None.

Charter and Bulk Fare
Italy is a major charter destination, especially from the East Coast.
Charters and bulk fares to Milan this year will probably be about
$500 to $600 from the East Coast, $600 to $700 from Chicago and
Texas, and $750 to $850 from the West Coast.

Munich

Major Airlines

	Round-trip fare to Munich from			
Fare Basis	New York	Chicago	Texas	West Coast
Cheapest excursion	$ 811	$ 878	$ 768	$ 972
Full fare				
Economy	1,652	1,780	1,816	1,964
Business Class	1,776	2,140	1,978	2,390
First Class	3,250	3,644	3,644	4,200

Restrictions on Lowest Available Fare
Peak season: June 1–September 14
Advance purchase: 21 days
Minimum stay: 7 days
Weekend supplement: approximately $50
Stopovers: none
Children's fare: 67%
Cancellation penalty: $75

Low-Fare Airlines
None.

Charter and Bulk Fare

Germany is an extremely active charter and bulk-fare destination, with big programs on its two charter airlines, Condor and LTU, as well as on U.S. carriers.

Nice

Major Airlines

Fare Basis	Round-trip fare to Nice from			
	New York	Chicago	Texas	West Coast
Cheapest excursion	$ 788	$ 898	$ 916	$ 971
Full fare				
Economy	1,838	1,966	2,002	2,178
Business Class	2,128	2,572	2,330	3,038
First Class	3,710	4,360	4,390	5,072

Restrictions on Lowest Available Fare

Peak season: May 15–September 30
Advance purchase: 21 days
Minimum stay: 7 days
Weekend supplement: $100 round-trip ($50 each way)
Stopovers: none
Children's fare: 67%
Cancellation penalty: $75

Comments: Lowest available fares to France from U.S. cities other than New York have generally been about $100 higher than fares to other European destinations of comparable distance. New York fares have been more competitive.

Low-Fare Airlines

There are no low-fare airlines presently serving Nice, and none is expected to do so in the near future. Icelandair offers low fares in conjunction with Luxair (via Luxembourg).

Charter and Bulk Fare

Air Charter, a subsidiary of Air France, and Tower offered charter service from New York in 1987 in the $500 to $600 range. Bulk fares from New York should be about $500, from Chicago $650, from Texas $675, and from the West Coast $775.

Oslo

Major Airlines

	Round-trip fare to Oslo from			
Fare Basis	New York	Chicago	Texas	West Coast
Cheapest excursion	$ 875	$ 985	$1,003	$1,085
Full fare				
Economy	1,556	1,770	2,224	2,304
Business Class	1,556	1,770	2,224	2,304
First Class	3,582	3,628	4,450	4,166

Restrictions on Lowest Available Fare
Peak season: June 1–August 14
Advance purchase: 21 days
Minimum stay: 10 days
Weekend supplement: $50 each way
Stopovers: none
Children's fare: 67%
Cancellation penalty: $75
Other special conditions: Ticketing required at time of reservation

Comments: Look for fares to Scandinavia to remain higher than airfares to other European destinations of comparable distance.

Low-Fare Airlines
Low-fare airline service to Oslo is unlikely.

Charter and Bulk Fare
Scandinavia has permitted only a trickle of charter service from the United States. You probably won't see much in 1988. Dedicated low-fare travelers will have to try nearby gateways—especially Frankfurt and Hamburg. Some bulk fares were available in 1987: New York $538, Chicago and Texas $738, and West Coast $758.

Paris

Major Airlines

	Round-trip fare to Paris from			
Fare Basis	New York	Chicago	Texas	West Coast
Cheapest excursion	$ 667	$ 777	$ 858	$ 922
Full fare				
Economy	1,654	1,782	1,818	1,994
Business Class	1,944	2,246	2,274	2,464
First Class	3,562	3,970	3,808	4,586
Concorde	4,296	—	—	—

Restrictions on Lowest Available Fare
Peak season: May 15–September 30
Advance purchase: 21 days
Minimum stay: 7 days
Weekend supplement: $100 round-trip ($50 each way)
Stopovers: none
Children's fare: 67%
Cancellation penalty: $75
Other special conditions: Indicated lowest fares require ticketing at
the time reservations are made. Where this is impractical, ordinary
APEX is available at $30 to $50 higher, depending on departure city.

Comments: Lowest available fares to France from U.S. cities
other than New York have generally been about $100 higher than
fares to other European destinations of comparable distances,
while New York fares have been more competitive. This pattern is
expected to continue this summer.

Low-Fare Airlines
At present, no low-fare airlines operate from the United States to
France. Icelandair offers very low through fares in conjunction
with Luxair (via Luxembourg).

Charter and Bulk Fare
Charters and bulk-fare seats are available. Look for direct charters
from several U.S. cities, although some of the biggest programs
will involve a domestic connection to a charter originating in New

York. Typical peak-season fares will be $500 to $600 from New York and $700 to $800 from the West Coast. Bulk fares as low as $438 from New York and $718 from the West Coast were available in 1987.

Rome

Major Airlines

| | Round-trip fare to Rome from | | | |
Fare Basis	New York	Chicago	Texas	West Coast
Cheapest excursion	$ 889	$ 989	$1,017	$1,072
Full fare				
Economy	1,510	1,710	1,674	1,872
Business Class	2,260	2,560	2,462	3,044
First Class	4,082	4,712	4,762	5,258

Restrictions on Lowest Available Fare
Peak season: June 1–September 14
Advance purchase: 21 days
Minimum stay: 7 days
Weekend stay: 7 days
Weekend supplement: $35 each way
Stopovers: none; open-jaw permitted
Children's fare: 67%
Cancellation penalty: $75

Low-Fare Airlines
None.

Charter and Bulk Fare
Italy is a major charter destination, especially from the East Coast. Last summer, programs operated from Boston, New York, and Philadelphia. Bulk fares and charters to Rome will probably be about $550 to $650 from the East Coast, $700 to $800 from Chicago and Texas, and $800 to $900 from the West Coast.

Shannon

Major Airlines

	Round-trip fare to Shannon from			
Fare Basis	New York	Chicago	Texas	West Coast
Cheapest excursion	$ 599	$ 699	$ 668	$ 782
Full fare				
Economy	—	—	—	—
Business Class	1,470	1,864	1,654	2,364
First Class	2,800	2,792	3,120	3,292

Restrictions on Lowest Available Fare
Peak season: June 1–September 14
Advance purchase: 21 days
Minimum stay: 7 days
Weekend supplement: $25 each way (except New York)
Stopovers: one at a U.S. gateway
Children's fare: 67%
Cancellation penalty: $50
Other special conditions: $100 for one change

Low-Fare Airlines
None.

Charter and Bulk Fare
Ireland has enjoyed good charter service over the years, and 1988 should see a repeat. Look for peak-season, round-trip fares of around $425 to $500 from the East Coast.

Stockholm

Major Airlines

	Round-trip fare to Stockholm from			
Fare Basis	New York	Chicago	Texas	West Coast
Cheapest excursion	$ 945	$1,055	$1,073	$1,149
Full fare				
Economy	1,696	1,910	2,364	2,446
Business Class	1,696	1,910	2,364	2,446
First Class	3,794	3,840	4,622	4,378

Restrictions on Lowest Available Fare
Peak season: June 1–August 14
Advance purchase: 21 days
Minimum stay: 10 days
Weekend supplement: $50 each way
Stopovers: none
Children's fare: 67%
Cancellation penalty: $75

Comments: Look for fares to Scandinavia to remain higher than airfares to other European destinations of comparable distance.

Low-Fare Airlines
None.

Charter and Bulk Fare
Scandinavia has permitted only a trickle of charter service from the United States. You probably won't see much activity in 1988. There's no market for low-fare airlines either. Dedicated low-fare travelers will have to try nearby gateways—especially Frankfurt and Hamburg. Bulk fares in 1987 were as low as $538 from New York, $738 from Chicago and Texas, and $858 from the West Coast.

Tel Aviv

Major Airlines

Fare Basis	Round-trip fare to Tel Aviv from			
	New York	Chicago	Texas	West Coast
Cheapest excursion	$ 919	$1,274	$1,117	$1,172
Full fare				
Economy	1,498	1,626	1,662	1,838
Business Class	2,958	3,402	3,288	3,868
First Class	4,422	5,072	5,102	5,784

Restrictions on Lowest Available Fare
Peak season: June 13–August 23
Advance purchase: 14 days
Minimum stay: 6 days
Weekend supplement: none
Stopovers: one free in Europe and one free at U.S. gateway

Children's fare: 75%
Cancellation penalty: $100

Low-Fare Airlines
Tower Air is pushing service to Israel. It is currently quoting an $800 round-trip fare from New York in the peak season. New York to Tel Aviv has always been a very competitive route, and it should remain so in summer 1988.

Charter and Bulk Fare
Israel has traditionally been a reasonably good market, but the low-fare airlines seem to be providing most of the cheaper opportunities on a scheduled (and possibly bulk-fare) basis rather than charter. Still, you can expect some flights, and at the same prices as the low-fare lines. In 1987, bulk fares were $650 to $800 from New York and $882 from the West Coast.

Vienna

Major Airlines

| Fare Basis | Round-trip fare to Vienna from | | | |
	New York	Chicago	Texas	West Coast
Cheapest excursion	$ 844	$ 954	$ 972	$1,027
Full fare				
Economy	1,458	1,958	1,760	1,760
Business Class	1,978	2,478	2,066	2,774
First Class	3,446	4,196	4,126	4,808

Restrictions on Lowest Available Fare
Peak season: June 1–September 14
Advance purchase: 21 days
Minimum stay: 7 days
Weekend supplement: $30 (Friday, Saturday, Sunday)
Stopovers: none
Children's fare: 67%
Cancellation penalty: $75
Other special conditions: $100 to change return date

Low-Fare Airlines

There has been no low-fare airline to Vienna, and none is likely this year. Tarom, the Romanian airline, offered a $225 one-way standby fare in 1987.

Charter and Bulk Fare

Over the past few years, sporadic charter programs have been operated to Vienna. 1987's low-price action was either with bulk fares or with group tour rates on Tarom. You can expect the same this year—few charters but several comparable low-cost options. In 1987, bulk fares were about $600 from New York and $748 from the West Coast.

Zurich

Major Airlines

Fare Basis	Round-trip fare to Zurich from			
	New York	Chicago	Texas	West Coast
Cheapest excursion	$ 776	$ 844	$ 904	$ 959
Full fare				
Economy	1,506	1,694	—	—
Business Class	1,694	1,916	1,896	2,604
First Class	3,228	3,614	3,980	4,590

Restrictions on Lowest Available Fare

Peak season: June 1–September 14
Advance purchase: 21 days
Minimum stay: 7 days
Weekend supplement: $100 round-trip ($50 each way)
Stopovers: none
Children's fare: 67%
Cancellation penalty: $75

Low-Fare Airlines

None.

Charter and Bulk Fare

Several operators plan to offer low-cost charters to Switzerland this summer, serving both Geneva and Zurich. Peak-season bulk and charter round-trip fares should be about $500 to $600 from New York, $650 from Chicago and Texas, and $800 to $900 from the West Coast.

PART II

Getting Around Europe

12

Internal European
Transportation
Options

If you're going to spend your entire European vacation exploring a single city, you don't need to worry about travel within Europe. You can skip this and the next three chapters. But most travelers visit at least two cities or regions on their trips. Chances are you're interested in knowing about the most efficient and pleasant ways to travel from place to place.

Getting around in Europe generally means using some combination of three alternatives: flying, taking trains, or driving in a rented car—the latter two in combination with a few boat or ferry trips to get across some of the channels and seas. Perhaps you'll take a few bus trips as well, but mainly for short, local excursions. The European countries have emphasized railroads rather than buses as the basic form of public surface travel. As with transatlantic air travel, your choices of internal transportation in Europe will be discussed in terms of cost, convenience, comfort, and contingency factors.

COST COMPARISONS

A good way to compare the costs of traveling around Europe by different methods is to compare per-person costs of some "standard" itineraries that are typical of trips that Americans might take:

- A 21-day trip of 1,500 miles, or about 70 miles a day on average, typical of a fairly intensive exploration within a single country or smaller multicountry region. Frankfurt-Zurich-Paris-Frankfurt, with a generous allowance for side-trip sightseeing excursions, is a good example.
- A 21-day trip of 3,000 miles, or about 140 miles a day on average, typical of a see-as-much-as-you-can multicountry trip. A trip from Amsterdam to Naples and back, with liberal allowance for sightseeing excursions, would be representative.
- A 60-day trip of 3,000 miles, or about 50 miles a day on average, typical of an all-summer stay that minimizes long-distance travel.
- A 60-day trip of 8,000 miles, typical of a multicountry trip that gets you to most of Europe's high spots over the course of a full summer.

Costs for these trips by the three major modes—rental car, rail, and air—are shown in the following table.

Table 4   European Transportation Costs (U.S. dollars)

Means of travel	21 days 1,500 mi.	21 days 3,000 mi.	60 days 3,000 mi.	60 days 8,000 mi.
Subcompact car, two people				
Rental/lease	$ 500	$ 500	$ 900	$ 900
Operations at 10¢/mi.	150	300	300	800
Trip cost				
Total	650	800	1,200	1,700
Per person	325	400	600	850
Per person per day	15	19	10	14
Midsize car, four people				
Rental/lease	$ 860	$ 860	$1,100	$1,100
Operations at 14¢/mi.	225	450	450	1,200
Trip cost				
Total	1,085	1,310	1,550	2,300
Per person	271	328	388	575
Per person per day	13	16	6	10
Rail (Eurailpass)				
Trip cost				
Per person	$ 370	$ 370	$ 650	$ 650
Per person per day	18	18	11	11

Table 4   European Transportation Costs (U.S. dollars)—*Continued*

Rail (Individual ticket)				
Trip cost (Second Class)				
Per person	$ 240	$ 480	$ 480	$1,280
Per person per day	11	23	8	21
Trip cost (First Class)				
Per person	$ 375	$ 750	$ 750	$2,000
Per person per day	18	36	13	33
Air Travel				
Trip cost (Economy)				
Per Person	$ 600	$1,200	$1,200	$2,400
Per person per day	29	57	20	40

Rental-Car Costs

Estimates of car-rental costs in the figures presented here are based on the least-expensive car rentals available from one or more of the 11 major European car-rental companies. The figures reflect renting a car at summer 1987 rates in one of the European countries with the lowest overall car-rental costs. In the two-month trips, automobile costs are based on use of one of the lowest-priced leases. Costs for the subcompact car are for a *standard* subcompact, as defined in chapter 14—something like a Ford Fiesta or Renault 5 le Car. Costs for the midsize car are based on a four-door model of a Ford Sierra, Opel Ascona, or Volkswagen Passat. The cost calculations used to derive the figure *include* collision-damage waiver (CDW) expenses estimated at $8 a day—even though it's optional, most Americans driving in Europe buy it. Expect rates to be up about 10 percent this summer.

The costs of operating a car in Europe are higher than at home, largely because gasoline costs up to $3 a gallon in Europe. European automobiles continue to use leaded high-octane gasoline to power high-compression engines, without clean-air modifications required in the United States, so fuel economy tends to be somewhat better than here. Even so, costs are well above those in the United States. Data reflected in the figures are based on operating costs of 10¢ a mile for a subcompact and 15¢ a mile for a four-passenger car.

Some additional costs in driving are not incorporated into the cost-comparison calculations. As at home, parking may be the biggest single expense. Very few downtown European hotels have free parking; many have none at all, and parking your car in a garage can easily add at least $5 to $10 a day to your transportation costs. You'll have trouble parking free or at nominal cost at the main city-center tourist attractions as well. And even off-the-beaten-track cities have discovered parking meters.

A second additional cost becomes apparent as soon as you hit the open road. The major highways in France, Italy, and Spain are toll roads, and, as on big turnpikes in the eastern United States, those tolls can add up to some hefty totals on long trips. Also, you'll find no shortage of toll bridges and tunnels in many European countries.

Rail Costs

Rail-cost estimates in the figures are shown both for Eurailpass and for individual tickets, estimated at 16¢ a mile in Second Class and 25¢ a mile in First Class. These average costs are typical of the railroad-ticket rates in the larger of the main tourist countries: Austria, Denmark, France, Germany, Italy, and the United Kingdom. Costs are substantially lower in several other European countries. Also, the use of passes limited to single countries sometimes results in still lower trip costs.

Three additional costs of rail travel are not incorporated into these calculations.

First, rail passes or ordinary tickets do not usually cover local transportation costs once you've arrived in a city. So you must plan on either municipal transit or taxis for travel between rail stations and hotels and for local sightseeing trips.

Second, train travelers tend to stay at city-center hotels and eat at downtown restaurants convenient to train stations. Almost universally, city hotel accommodations are substantially more expensive than comparable-quality accommodations in the countryside. When you're budgeting, you should generally figure on spending $5 to $25 per person per day more (depending on your standards and the area in which you'll be traveling) for accommodations and meals when you travel by train than when you drive a rented car.

Third, you have to pay a fee of at least $1 to reserve a seat on the main express trains. Some of the best trains also require a ticket surcharge. You must pay these extra fees separately whether you are using individual tickets, Eurailpass, or a national unlimited mileage pass.

Air-Travel Costs

The air-travel cost estimates in the figures are especially soft. They're based on typical costs of around 40¢ a mile for the short trips and 30¢ a mile for the 3,000- and 8,000-mile trips. But the fares for any individual trip can differ substantially from these averages, depending on route, length of stay, and which of a bewildering variety of special ticket deals you might find available for each itinerary.

The additional costs of air travel, beyond the ticket, are similar to those of rail travel, though potentially larger. Access to and from airports by special bus, train, or taxi can easily add $5 to $30 a person every time you move from one city to the next.

CONVENIENCE FACTORS

Some of the most successful U.S. guidebook writers recommend train travel as the most convenient way to see Europe, as well as the most economical. Express trains run on most of the main routes every hour during the day, and many of these trains run through some of Europe's most scenic areas. You can get a close look at the countryside without keeping your eyes on the road, coping with unfamiliar roads and traffic patterns, or worrying about taking a wrong turn. You arrive and depart right in the center of most cities—no fighting city and suburban traffic to get out of town, and no hassles about buses to the airport. And rail travel is fast. Express trains almost everywhere zip along at 70 to 90 miles an hour, and the high-tech French TGV and the British HST cruise at 125 to 160 miles an hour.

Rail travel has some experiential drawbacks, however. You can't have the train stop while you take a few pictures of that spectacular scene you just passed or have the train wait for you to explore an interesting castle or church. You'll miss the joys of the smaller villages and of staying in countryside hotels or resorts that may be well off the beaten track; you won't have the chance to have that delightful meal in an inexpensive country inn.

Driving a rented car, for many, is the ideal way to travel through Europe. You can stop whenever you wish. You can change your plans on impulse to explore intriguing sights that you may encounter. And traveling by car allows you to get off the beaten track, to adventure and explore a region in depth. Your luggage can remain in the trunk much of the time; you're not obliged to handle all your belongings every time you move to a new city. And you can enjoy dining and staying overnight in country inns or picnicking in scenic locales—special experiences that may save you money, too.

Driving really isn't a very good way to travel if you're staying mainly in the bigger cities. The benefits of flexibility generally don't compensate adequately for the hassles of trying to cope with traffic and parking. And even in the countryside, where driving is most advantageous, touring Americans can sometimes run into considerable difficulties if they get lost or need some mechanical assistance in a small community where no one speaks English.

Speed is the main advantage of flying as a means of getting around Europe. It's probably the only advantage and, in many cases, not a very important one. When you consider the extra time of getting to and from airports, plus the requirement that you be at the airport at least an hour before flight time for most international services, you find that an express train is competitive with flying for total elapsed time, city center to city center or door-to-door, for trips of 300 miles or less. However, if your itinerary calls for visits to a few points that are widely separated, or requires you to get across one or more of the seas, the airplane may be your only practical alternative. For example, if your trip consists of visits to London and Athens, or Copenhagen, Helsinki, and Rome, you almost have to fly. Even the fastest surface travel could eat up two or three days for each leg of your journey.

COMFORT FACTORS

The comfort implications of driving, pro and con, are essentially the same in Europe as at home, at least in terms of physical comfort. "Mental" comfort may be another question. Some Americans are apprehensive about driving in unfamiliar circumstances, and driving along a narrow country lane used by oxcarts as much as by automobiles can be unfamiliar to many. Also, a driver accustomed to speed limits of 55 to 60 miles per hour on U.S. interstate highways may be intimidated by a steady stream of big Mercedes sedans cruising along at 90 to 100, flashing their headlights at anyone timid enough to be moving more slowly. But the adjustment is easier than many might think. Traffic signs throughout Europe use

The Budapest Connection

Last year, *Consumer Reports Travel Letter* publicized a little-known bargain in internal European air travel. For $299 per person (double occupancy), the Holiday in Budapest package offered by Malev (the Hungarian national airline) provides three nights in a good Budapest hotel plus round-trip airfare from any of Malev's 14 gateway cities in western Europe: Amsterdam, Athens, Barcelona, Brussels, Copenhagen, Frankfurt, Helsinki, London, Madrid, Milan, Munich, Paris, Rome, and Zurich. The single supplement is $45; you can upgrade to deluxe hotels and extend your stay at modest cost.

The special feature of this package is that *it's available on an open-jaw basis:* For the standard price of $299 per person, you can fly to Budapest from one western-European city and return to another. Thus, if your European itinerary includes two of the 14 cities served by Malev, the Budapest excursion can take the place of a direct trip between the two cities. And the total cost, including both airfare and hotel, is lower than the lowest available one-way airfare between many of the 14 gateways. Incidentally, you'll find Budapest a fascinating and inexpensive place to spend a few days.

---

the same international pictorial symbols that require no special language capability, direction signs are at least as good as those at home, European road maps are excellent, and European gas stations and garages are pretty well accustomed to serving American visitors in their rental cars.

European rail travel is generally quite comfortable, especially on the main through-express services. Even Second Class provides wider seats and more legroom than Coach or Economy air service, and First Class train seats are very roomy and comfortable. During peak travel periods, however, Second Class trains can get very full, to the point that aisles are crammed with standees, and Second Class comfort standards in Greece, Italy, and Spain leave a lot to be desired at any time.

Intra-European air services are similar to those in the United States. Seats, however, can be even less comfortable than on domestic U.S. services.

CONTINGENCIES

There's not much to say about contingencies that you don't already know. Especially in the summer, drivers don't have to worry much about snowbound mountain passes or washed-away bridges. The trains and planes run like clockwork—except when there's a strike. All in all, you can pretty well count on making your targeted itineraries by any of the modes.

Theft of luggage, cameras, and other personal valuables can be a problem in both cars and trains. Luggage and valuables are not necessarily secure in the trunk of your car: Rental cars (with their company decals) are too often the targets of thieves who are very skilled at opening car locks. There have also been frequent reports of pickpockets plying their trade on European trains. Travelers trying to get some sleep on overnight trips are especially vulnerable, as are Americans, who seem to be easy to identify and who are apparently considered especially inviting targets.

YOUR BEST DEAL

The detailed comparisons between car, rail, and air demonstrate some overall points:

- Rail and rental cars are generally competitive in cost for a wide variety of trips. Eurailpass has the edge for the high-mileage trips; four people sharing a car can travel very inexpensively for most trip itineraries.
- Individual tickets—rather than Eurailpass—are considerably less expensive for trips with a low average daily mileage, especially if you're willing to travel Second Class.
- Rail is about the only economically practical way for the single traveler to get around in Europe.
- Traveling around Europe by air is competitive only for those rare cases when you travel for relatively short distances during long periods of stay or if you're visiting a few widely spaced points. For most other types of trips, flying is substantially more expensive.

For most travelers, the practical choice is between rail and car. Since the costs are generally competitive, the decision hinges on the travel style that suits you best:

- Rent a car if you're interested in seeing a lot of the countryside and enjoy almost total flexibility in where and when you go.
- Use the train if you're concentrating mainly on visits to Europe's bigger cities or if driving in a foreign country makes you apprehensive or if you're traveling by yourself.

USE A VARIETY OF METHODS

If you elect to use Eurailpass or a single-country rail pass or to rent a car, you're pretty much committed to that method of travel throughout your visit. After all, if you're paying for unlimited mileage, the more you use, the less each mile costs. But you don't have to settle for just one form of transportation, especially if your trip mainly consists of visits to a few of the bigger cities. After all, you don't need a car or a rail pass when you're exploring a major city. Instead, you might consider individually purchased train tickets for your longer hauls. Then, for special excursions outside major cities, you can rent cars for the days that you actually need them. Although daily rentals are more expensive per day than weekly rentals, the total cost should be much lower if you just rent for a few individual days.

DON'T BE TOO FRUGAL

Finally, when it comes to internal transportation in Europe, experienced travelers know that trying to shave every last dollar off the final cost is often false economy. It simply doesn't make sense to try to stuff more than two adults and one medium-sized or two small children into a typical European subcompact car. For all the time you spend driving, a few extra dollars spent on a slightly larger car will pay handsome dividends in more comfort and less stress for all concerned.

Similarly, traveling through Europe by train is perhaps the one time even dedicated money savers should consider First Class. It's hard to justify a First Class airfare premium of, for example, $1,000 for an eight-hour trip: $125 an hour is a very stiff price to pay for a more comfortable seat and a few drinks. But on a two-week German rail pass, for example, the difference between First and Second Class is $55. You could probably travel at least 1,500 miles with this pass, so at an average of 50 miles an hour, you'd be riding trains for thirty hours. Thus the premium for First Class amounts to less than $2 an hour, a reasonable price for the genuine roominess and comfort of First Class travel.

13

Rail Travel

Travel around Europe by train is a most satisfying way to get where you're going.

About the only rail service in the United States that comes close to European standards of speed and schedule convenience is in the Northeast Corridor between Boston and Washington. In western Europe, almost all main intercity corridors enjoy rail service that's almost as fast as the Metroliner, operates more frequently, and is better maintained. Many countries have achieved a standard of one fast train per hour on major trunk routes and more frequently scheduled local and branch-line service.

There are three basic ways you can buy rail transportation within Europe. Eurailpass and the comparable BritRail Pass are best known. These tickets provide unlimited rail travel throughout Europe and throughout Britain, respectively, for a set number of days; the British term *rover* is a particularly suitable name for them. But there are quite a few other types of individual-country rover tickets as well that may suit you better. Finally, you can buy individual tickets for your trips as you need them.

EURAILPASS

Eurailpass, the best-known European rail ticket, is available for First Class only:

First Class

15 days	$298		
21 days	$370	2 months	$650
1 month	$470	3 months	$798

Children under 12 years old pay half fare. Children under four travel free.

The Eurail Saverpass for two or more people traveling together costs $210 per person for First Class off-season (October to May). It is limited to 15 days of consecutive travel. During the peak season (June to September), three or more people must travel together; the cost is $210 each.

The new Eurail Flexipass, good for nine days of travel within a twenty-one-day period, is $310.

A Eurail Youthpass for travelers under 26 provides for one month of unlimited Second Class travel for $320 or two months for $420.

These Eurailpass tickets offer unlimited rail travel on the national railroad systems of 16 countries: Austria, Belgium, Denmark, Finland, France, Greece, Ireland, Italy, Luxembourg, the Netherlands, Norway, Portugal, Spain, Sweden, Switzerland, and West Germany. In addition, they allow free or reduced-cost travel on many specialized railways, buses, and ferries or steamers—most notably the services from Brindisi (Italy) to Patras (Greece); Cherbourg and Le Havre (France) to Cork and Rosslare (Ireland); and Stockholm to Turku and Helsinki (Finland), and the links between Denmark and Sweden. They also qualify the holder for discounts on a number of other travel services. There is an $8 high-season supplement on steamers between Brindisi and Patras.

Reservations should be made in advance for all rail journeys, since seats can sell out quickly in the summer.

The Eurailpass system has two main gaps in areas served. It does not include Great Britain (England, Scotland, and Wales) or Yugoslavia—which means that Greece can be reached with Eurailpass only by steamer.

Eurailpass prices are established in U.S. dollars and are not subject to change due to exchange-rate fluctuations. You have to buy your tickets before you reach Europe. The pound-priced versions sold in Great Britain offer no bargains for U.S. travelers.

A Eurailpass is easy to buy and easy to use. Any travel agent can get one for you.

INDIVIDUAL COUNTRY ROVERS

Most European countries have individual rovers (usually both First and Second Class versions) valid only within their own systems, and several adjacent countries have regional multicountry rovers. BritRail is the best known because it's usually sold as the complement to Eurailpass for travel in Great Britain.

Individual national rovers are less expensive than Eurailpass for First Class travel and significantly less expensive for travelers willing to ride Second Class, an option not available to adults on Eurailpass. Most countries also have quite a few other rovers and special tickets.

INDIVIDUAL TICKETS

Eurailpass, BritRail Pass, and the other rovers are widely publicized. U.S. travel agents find them easy to sell. But rovers are not always the best way to buy European rail travel. Your best rail deal depends mainly on the number of miles you'll be traveling. If you're going to travel extensively in several countries, Eurailpass is likely to be your best deal, but the individual country rovers are great for extensive exploration of single countries. If your total trip mileage will be fairly limited, however, it's often much cheaper simply to buy individual tickets for individual trips. Basically, you have to determine whether Eurailpass is really a good deal on the basis of how much you plan to use it.

For example, figuring the average cost for First Class rail travel for a two-week trip among the Eurailpass countries at around 25¢ a mile, you'd have to travel 1,500 miles or more on individual tickets to equal the $370 Eurailpass price. If you're willing to travel Second Class, at an average fare of about 16¢ a mile, your break-even point would be something like 2,300 miles. If your itinerary calls for substantially less travel, you're better off buying individual tickets.

The individual country rover in Germany isn't much cheaper than Eurailpass for First Class travel. Its main advantages are the Second Class option and availability for shorter time periods. But the Italian, Austrian, Benelux, French, Swiss, and Scandinavian rovers can be considerably less expensive than Eurailpass for both First and Second Class travel if you're staying within a single country or region.

Of course, break-even points calculated with average per-mile costs are just for general guidance. For a precise determination, you have to compare costs for your individual trip. It's really quite easy. You can approximate your total mileage from maps. Or, if you're really interested in detail, the Thomas Cook *Continental Timetable*, available in U.S. travel bookstores, shows exact point-to-point rail distances (in kilometers, which you then divide by 1.61 to convert to miles). Use the figures on page 127 to estimate the total cost of your trip with individual tickets and compare this total with the cost of one or more rover tickets that would cover your trip.

The following railfare listings should give you the information for each country so you can figure the most economical way to buy your tickets.

BUYING RAIL TICKETS

You have to buy Eurailpasses and BritRail passes before you arrive in continental Europe, and you have to buy some other single and multicountry unlimited mileage rover tickets before you arrive in the country or countries in which you'll use them. You can buy them either through your travel agent or directly from the various national tourist offices or national railroad offices in the United States. In the listings that follow, prices for rovers available in the United States are given in U.S. dollars. Those rover passes available only in Europe are given in local currency because dollar prices fluctuate.

Regional rover tickets and a few of the national rovers can be bought after you arrive. It's probably better to buy these tickets when you're ready to use them rather than beforehand, so that you can choose the options that best suit your immediate needs. You can generally buy them at major-city railroad stations.

When you buy a ticket for international travel within Europe, you may find that some eligibility requirements (especially for children's half-fare tickets) are quite different from those for travel entirely within the country where your trip originates. Check these specific rules carefully before you buy tickets.

Many of the best rail-ticket programs require some sort of proof of foreign residence, age, or status. Your U.S. passport will serve in most cases. Students may be required to show additional identification. If you're a student, check with your local registration office for some sort of official ID.

Finally, you'll note that most of the special youth deals are available only for Second Class travel. Family groups that include both adults and youths who want to travel together on Eurailpass will therefore have to buy regular adult Eurailpasses for the youths as well as the adults—or else the adults will have to ride in Second Class, even though they've paid for First.

European trains sometimes consist of several parts that at some point split and go to several different destinations. However, individual cars are always clearly marked, and the ticket inspectors take care to inform passengers if they are in the wrong car for their desired destination.

The rates given are the latest provided by the individual countries in mid-1987.

Austria

Unlimited Mileage Passes

Type of ticket or pass	Valid for	Cost (schillings)	
		First Class	Second Class
Network pass (*Bundenetzkarte*)	9 days	S2,160	S1,440
	16 days	2,940	1,960
	30 days	4,650	2,940
Youth ticket	9 days	—	950
	16 days	—	1,350
Provincial ticket	9 days	72	48
	16 days	105	70
	30 days	162	108

Conversion rate, mid-1987: S12.75 = $1

The Network Pass can be bought in Frankfurt, Munich, and Zurich. The Austria Ticket for travelers under 26 can also be used on government post buses. Both tickets allow discounts of 50 percent on DDSG steamships (on the Danube, for example) and mountain cog railways.

The Provincial Ticket, a regional rover pass good for travel in any one of the nine individual provinces, is obtainable only in Austria.

Other Special Tickets and Passes

Kilometric tickets for Second Class rail travel may be good buys for families. Basically, you multiply the distance you plan to travel by the number of people in your party and buy the appropriate kilometric ticket. A 2,000-kilometer ticket costs S1,700; a 5,000-kilometric ticket, S4,100; a 10,000-kilometer ticket, S8,000. Seniors (women over sixty, men over sixty-five) can buy a pass good for one calendar year for S160, which gives a 50 percent reduction on any ticket. Passport identification is required.

Children under the age of six travel free; those 6 to 15 travel at half fare.

Comment: If you want to travel from one part of Austria to another on a corridor that crosses Italian or German territory, try to travel on a *Korridorzuge* (corridor train). These trains cross frontiers without the usual passport formalities because they do not board or discharge passengers outside Austria.

Belgium

Unlimited Mileage Passes

Type of ticket or pass	Valid for	Cost (Belgian francs) First Class	Second Class
Benelux-Tourrail			
Adult	5/17 days	BF3,600	BF2,400
Youth (12–26)	5/17 days	2,680	1,800
Child (6–11)	5/17 days	1,800	1,200
Belgian-Tourrail			
16-day card	16 days	4,410	2,940
Adult	5/16 days	2,352	1,554
	8/16 days	3,108	2,058
Youth (12–26)	5/16 days	1,764	1,176
	8/16 days	2,310	1,554
Child (6–11)	5/16 days	1,176	798
	8/16 days	1,554	1,050
Half-fare card	1 month	756	504

Conversion rate, mid-1987: BF38 = $1

The Benelux-Tourrail pass covers travel in Belgium, the Netherlands, and Luxembourg. Belgian-Tourrail is confined to Belgium.

Both Benelux-Tourrail and Belgian-Tourrail can be used only on a specified number of days within a longer total time. In the validity notation used above, the number before the slash (/) indicates the number of days on which the ticket may be used, and the number after the slash indicates the total maximum validity period. For example, 5/16 indicates that a pass can be used on any 5 days during a 16-day period.

The Benelux-Tourrail can be bought in Belgium (as well as in the Netherlands and Luxembourg). It is valid only during the major tourist season: March 15 to September 15. The Belgian-Tourrail can be purchased only in Belgium and is valid March 15 to September 30 and December 15 to 30. Both require passport or other identification; youth and child passes require proof of age.

Half-fare cards, available year-round, allow a 50-percent discount on all rail travel within Belgium. The price is the same for all travelers.

Other Special Tickets and Passes

Inexpensive weekend excursion tickets, for example, to the Belgian beaches or to the Ardennes forest, are available for travel from Friday evening to Monday morning. Day excursion tickets to the same areas are available only during the summer. Benelux Weekend Tickets are special round-trip fares for long weekend trips to the other Benelux countries.

A Beautiful Day tickets offer reduced fares for excursions to local points of interest and include admission to museums, boating parks, etc.

Children under six travel free; those 6 to 12 pay half fare.

Denmark
Unlimited Mileage Passes

Type of ticket or pass	Valid for	Cost (Danish/Swedish krone) First Class	Second Class
Danish Rail Pass	1 month	DKr1,815	Dkr1,425
Scandinavian Rail Pass Nordtourist	21 days	SKr1,940	Skr1,295

Conversion rate, mid-1987: DKr6.97 = $1; SKr6.37 = $1

The Danish Rail Pass, available only in Denmark, is good for one month's unlimited travel on Danish State Railways (DSB). A half-fare pass is available for children under twelve.

The Scandinavian Rail Pass, called *Nordtourist*, permits unlimited rail travel in Denmark, Finland, Norway, and Sweden. It is available in the United States and at Scandinavian rail stations. The ticket is also valid on many ferries. It allows a 50-percent reduction on others. Cabin rates are additional on boats. The pass also provides for discounts at more than 100 first-class hotels June 1 to September 1.

Other Special Tickets and Passes

Seniors can travel for half fares during off-peak periods, for round-trip tickets only; an identification card is issued at stations. These tickets cannot be used from 2:00 to 7:00 P.M. Friday, from 8:00 A.M. to noon Saturday, and from 2:00 P.M. to midnight Sunday and some holidays.

Groups (minimum two adults and one child) can travel at a reduction of 30 percent or more on individual fares. The discounts vary from midweek (more) to weekends (less) and according to the number of persons traveling together.

Children under four travel free; those 4 to 12 pay half fare.

Comment: Because Denmark is small and flat, most train trips are no more than commuter runs. Rail stations also sell tickets for connecting ferries and buses. Seat reservations are generally required on longer trips. Reservations are essential for all services using the Great Belt Ferry.

France

Unlimited Mileage Passes

Type of ticket or pass	Valid for	Cost (U.S. dollars) First Class	Second Class
France Railpass	4/15 days	$ 89	$ 69
	9/30 days	190	130
	16/30 days	250	170
France Saverpass (for two people)	9 days	$299	$199

The France Railpass consists of coupons for four, nine, or sixteen nonconsecutive days of rail travel to be used within a 15-day (for the four-day pass) or 30-day period, and good on First or Second Class service. It includes bus service between Paris airports and downtown Paris, a limited Metropass for holders of nine- and 16-day passes, and discounts on various attractions and museums throughout France. You can buy the France Railpass in the United States.

Other Special Tickets and Passes

The *Carte Jeune* and *Carré Jeune* both offer 50-percent reductions on fares on "blue days" (off-peak periods) to those 25 and under. Both cost approximately $22 and are valid for Second Class travel only. The *Carte* permits unlimited travel June 1 to September 30 and allows one free couchette (sleeper) on any route. The *Carré* allows four single uses at any time during the year. The suburban rail network around Paris is excluded from both passes. These passes can be purchased only in France.

Séjour return tickets offer a 25-percent discount off any return journey (to point of origin) totaling more than 1,000 kilometers with a five-day minimum-stay requirement between outbound and return trips. These tickets may be used only on "blue days."

Children under four travel free (provided they do not require a seat when the train is full); those 4 to 12 pay half fare.

Comment: The French boast the fastest train in the world. The *trains à grande vitesse* (TGVs) regularly reach speeds of 168 miles (270 kilometers) per hour. Traveling time between Lyons and Paris (265 miles) is two hours. There is a compulsory seat-reservation fee on the TGV of about $4.

The TGV is very cramped and spartan in Second Class. First Class is recommended for all but the most hardy. Buffet food is limited and expensive; the full meals are a better value but must be ordered at the time of booking.

West Germany

Unlimited Mileage Passes

Type of ticket or pass	Valid for	Cost (U.S. dollars)	
		First Class	Second Class
Tourist card	4 days	$110	$ 75
	9 days	170	115
	16 days	230	160
Youth card	9 days	—	75
(junior tourist card)	16 days	—	95

Both cards can be bought in the United States and in other countries in Europe but not in the Federal Republic itself. Purchasers must have a valid passport. Besides offering the user unlimited rail travel throughout the Federal Republic, they also provide:

- free motorcoach transportation on all routes of Europabus, including the "Romantic Road" and "Castle Road" routes, April to November
- free KD Rhineline sightseeing steamers traversing the Rhine, Main, and Moselle rivers, mid-April to mid-October
- reduced fares on rail travel to Berlin with a free city sightseeing tour and free transit visa to East Berlin (not available with the four-day card)

No supplement is paid on Intercity (IC) or fast trains.

The Youth Card or Junior Tourist Card for Second Class travel is available to those under 26. A valid passport with proof of age is required.

Other Special Tickets and Passes

Seniors (women over 60, men over 65) can buy a discount pass for DM110 allowing half-fare purchases throughout the system for one year. Proof of age is required. These passes are sold at German railway stations.

"Tramper" tickets allow unlimited Second Class travel for one month for travelers under 23, or for those under 27 with valid student identification. Travel without supplement on Intercity trains (ICs) is allowed. These tickets (DM245) are also sold only at German railway stations.

Tourenkarte (regional rail rovers) are available to travelers who also hold a rail ticket for a return journey in which the entire trip totals more than 250 kilometers each way. These tickets, which can be purchased only in Germany, provide for unlimited Second Class rail travel, including most buses, for 10 days within a period of 21 days in a particular region. They cost DM46 for one person, DM62 for two persons traveling together, and DM77 for a family traveling together with any number of children under 18.

A *Bezirkswochenkarte* (Weekly District Ticket) provides the same type of travel as the *Tourenkarte* but does not require the long-distance rail ticket. The cost is DM125 First Class, DM83 Second Class per person. Children 4 to 11 travel for half fare.

The "Rail and Fly" ticket for travelers holding a valid return airline ticket gives the user a reduced fare for the journey to and from the airport. The cost is DM140 First Class and DM90 Second Class. For two people traveling together the cost is DM210 for First Class and DM140 for Second Class; for each additional person the cost is DM70 for First Class and DM50 for Second Class. Children under 17 can ride on this ticket for DM35 in both classes. Children under four travel free; those 4 to 11 pay half fare.

Comment: GermanRail operates many Intercity (IC) trains that serve more than 50 cities within the Federal Republic, Austria, and the Netherlands. Many of these IC trains stop at Frankfurt airport. We've received reports of last-minute platform changes on main IC routes from those shown on the indicator boards. Check that you are on the right platform before boarding.

A supplement on tickets purchased in Germany of DM5, including seat reservation, is required on all Intercity trains, as is a supplement of DM3 on "D" trains for travel of less than 50 kilometers. If supplements are paid on the train, rather than at the ticket window, an additional DM1 is required. There is generally a charge for seat reservations.

Greece

Unlimited Mileage Passes

Type of ticket or pass	Valid for	First Class	Cost (drachmas) Second Class
Touring card	10 days	—	DR4,645
	20 days	—	7,620
	30 days	—	10,270

Conversion rate, mid-1987: Dr138 = $1

Touring cards can be obtained for unlimited Second Class travel on the Greek Railway Network and CH buses. Depending on the number of people traveling together, there may be a further discount off the rate quoted for the basic touring card.

Other Special Tickets and Passes

Senior cards are available to those 60 and over with a valid passport. They cost Dr4,975 for "A" class (or First Class) travel and Dr3,320 for "B" class (or Second Class) travel, allowing five one-way trips, except on certain dates around Christmas and Easter and during the summer (July to September). They also provide for a 50-percent reduction on all additional trips on the inland network and on CH buses.

Children under four travel free; those 4 to 12 pay half fare.

Comment: The main rail route into Greece is through Yugoslavia. International express trains enter the country via Belgrade. Because Yugoslavia is not part of the Eurail network, Eurailpass holders must travel via Italy and the ferry at Brindisi to reach Greece. Service from Athens to Salonika and from Athens to Corinth is adequate but poor by comparison with that in the rest of Europe.

Ireland

Unlimited Mileage Passes

Type of ticket or pass	Valid for	Cost (dollars) Standard Class
Rambler (rail only)	8/15 days	$ 73
	15/30 days	108
Rambler (rail and bus)	8/15 days	91
	15/30 days	133
Youth Rambler (rail and bus)	8/15 days	77
	15/30 days	103
	30 days	153
Irish Overlander (allows travel into Northern Ireland)	15/30 days	153

Ramblers (except youth) are available in the United States or Ireland. Youth Ramblers can be purchased in the United States through C.I.E. Tours International, 122 East 42nd Street, New York, NY 10168–0015. The bus and rail Rambler is usually a better value for traveling around the country, since buses and trains are more complementary than competitive.

The age limit on Youth Ramblers is 25; proof of age is required. Youth Ramblers may be purchased only in the United States and Canada.

Other Special Tickets or Passes
None. Children under 14 travel at half fare.

Comment: Rail service in the Republic of Ireland provides limited geographical coverage compared with that in most other European countries. Although all major cities are connected by rail, service does not extend into many scenic parts of the country.

Italy

Unlimited Mileage Passes

Type of ticket or pass	Valid for	Cost (U.S. dollars)	
		First Class	Second Class
Italian Unlimited Rail Pass	8 days	$134	$ 85
	15 days	164	103
	21 days	195	120
	30 days	238	150

The Italian Unlimited Rail Pass, also called the BTLC Italian Tourist Ticket, can be purchased outside Italy as well as in Rome and in border cities.

Other Special Tickets and Passes

The Italian kilometric ticket provides for 3,000 kilometers of travel in up to 20 trips, by as many as five people at one time. It is valid for two months. When the ticket is used simultaneously by more than one person, the distance traveled is multiplied by the number of users and the total deducted from the 3,000-kilometer limit. Kilometric tickets must be date-stamped. They cost $165 for First Class and $93 for Second Class. There is a supplementary charge for *Rapido* trains. The Italian Unlimited Rail Pass and the kilometric ticket can be bought in the United States through offices of Italian State Railways or in Italy at rail stations of principal cities.

Tourists are given a 15-percent discount on day-return tickets with a maximum distance traveled of 50 kilometers. A three-day return ticket is available, which grants the same discount on journeys of 250 kilometers traveled.

Family rates are given for members of a household (minimum three persons) traveling together. The reduction is about 20 percent for adults and 65 percent for children. Travel-at-Will tickets are available for children under 12 at half fare; children under four travel free.

Comment: Seat reservations are advisable. Rail service between the major Italian cities is fast, frequent, and relatively inexpensive.

The best *Rapido* services require a supplement over the individual ticket rates quoted calculated on distance traveled, at approximately 30 percent over the regular fare. Some offer only First Class.

Luxembourg

Unlimited Mileage Passes

Type of ticket or pass	Valid for	Cost (Lux. francs)	
		First Class	Second Class
Benelux-Tourrail			
Adult	5/17 days	LF3,600	LF2,400
Youth (12–26)	5/17 days	2,680	1,800
Child (6–11)	5/17 days	1,800	1,200
Network tickets	Weekend/holiday half fare on return		
	1 day	—	LF 200
	5 days	—	600
	1 month	—	1,600

Conversion rate, mid-1987: LF38 = $1

The Benelux-Tourrail pass covers rail travel in all Benelux countries—Luxembourg, the Netherlands, and Belgium. It can be purchased in Luxembourg at any railway station as well as in other Benelux countries. See the rail listing under Belgium for a discussion of valid dates.

Network tickets sold in Luxembourg are valid for unlimited travel on the Luxembourg National Railway and bus system.

Other Special Tickets and Passes
Seniors over 65 pay half fare for First and Second Class travel on trains and buses. Children 4 to 12 pay half fare; children under four on parent's lap travel free.

Comment: Luxembourg has an integrated rail and bus network operated by the Luxembourg National Railways.

Netherlands

Unlimited Mileage Passes

Type of ticket or pass	Valid for	Cost (U.S. dollars)	
		First Class	Second Class
Rail Ranger	3 days	$51	$34
	7 days	69	47
Benelux-Tourrail		(Dutch florins)	
Adult	5/17 days	Df173	Df124
Youth (12–26)	5/17 days	132	91
Child (6–11)	5/17 days	87	61

Conversion rate, mid-1987: Df12.03 = $1

The Rail Ranger is available in the Netherlands and from the Netherlands Board of Tourism Offices in New York and San Francisco. A photograph is required for the seven-day pass.

The Benelux-Tourrail pass covers travel in all Benelux countries. See the rail listing under Belgium for a discussion of valid dates.

Other Special Tickets and Passes

Public Transport Link Rover (an add-on to the Netherlands Pass) allows unlimited travel on all buses (except KLM Airport Bus), trams, and metros. It is available in the Netherlands or from the Netherlands Board of Tourism offices in New York and San Francisco. This pass costs $4 for three days or $8.50 for seven days. If purchased in the Netherlands, guilder (or florin) prices will differ.

Teenage Rovers, for those under 19, are available for unlimited Second Class travel on any four out of ten days for Df140. Family Rover tickets are also available for unlimited travel on any four out of ten days—First Class, Df1,200; Second Class, Df1,140.

Multi-Rover tickets are also available for a group of two to six persons traveling together for one day's unlimited travel in Second Class. They can be used weekdays after 9:00 A.M. and all day on weekends and holidays. They cost Df172 for two persons; Df187 for three persons, Df1101 for four persons, Df1115 for five persons, and Df1129 for six persons.

Seniors can purchase half-fare cards good for either three months or one year.

Children under four travel free; those four to nine travel at half fare.

Comment: The Netherlands has a sliding fare structure based on total distance traveled; 250 kilometers is about as far as you can go in Holland.

Norway

Unlimited Mileage Passes

Type of ticket or pass	Valid for	Cost (Nor. krone) First Class	Second Class
Norwegian Bargain Rail Pass	21 days	—	NKr270
		(U.S. dollars)	
Scandinavian Rail Pass	21 days	$280	$187

Conversion rate, mid-1987: NKr6.7 = $1

The Norwegian Bargain Rail Pass, which can be bought only in Norway, is good for travel on weekdays (except Friday) but not during the Easter and Christmas holiday periods. See the entry under Denmark in this chapter for complete information on the Scandinavian Rail Pass.

Other Special Tickets and Passes

Two or more persons can obtain reductions of 25 percent off regular rail fare on journeys of 100 kilometers or more.

Seniors over 67 pay half fare; younger spouses of a qualifying senior can also use these tickets. Proof of age is required. Identification cards are available at railway stations.

Children under four travel free; those 4 to 16 pay half fare. Those with international tickets pay half fare to age 12.

Comment: Norway's rail network offers some of Europe's most spectacular scenery. Trains often require reservations (obligatory on express). Seat reservations cost NKr12. It's a good idea to purchase tickets a day in advance for night trains leaving the country.

Portugal

Unlimited Mileage Passes

Type of ticket or pass	Valid for	Cost (escudos) First Class	Second Class
Tourist Ticket	7 days	Esc 7,225	—
	14 days	11,530	—
	21 days	16,470	—

Conversion rate, mid-1987: Esc143 = $1

This rover ticket is available for purchase in Portugal.

Other Special Tickets and Passes

Family tickets are available for a minimum of three persons: The first adult pays full fare; other family members pay half fares except children 4 to 11, who pay one-quarter fare. The age limit for off-spring is 18.

On standard tickets, children 4 to 12 pay half fare; children under four travel free.

Seniors (men 65 and over; women 60 and over) pay half fare with proof of age.

Comment: Seat reservations are mandatory on international trains and for Lisbon-Oporto and Lisbon-Algarve trains. Supplements are required on services classed as *Rapido,* but there are not many of them. Some stations in the Algarve are quite a distance from the center of the towns they serve. Train times should always be checked with the latest wall timetable at the station of departure; the standard international timetable references may not be accurate.

Spain

Unlimited Mileage Passes

Type of ticket or pass	Valid for	Cost (pesetas)	
		First Class	Second Class
Tarjeta Turista	8 days	Pts13,000	Pts 9,000
(tourist card)	15 days	21,000	15,000
	22 days	25,000	19,000

Conversion rate, mid-1987: Pts160 = $1

Tarjeta Turística (tourist ticket) can be purchased only in Spain at main railroad stations.

Other Special Tickets and Passes

Chéquetren is a special rail pass or voucher that can be purchased only in Spain at any main railway station or local travel agency. The pass can be used by a maximum of six people traveling together to gain a saving of 15 percent off normal fares. The pass can be purchased for about 21,250 to 29,750 pesetas.

Round-trip discounts are effective on "blue days" that the Spanish National Railways (RENFE) establishes at the beginning of the year. A copy of the calendar can be obtained at the information office of railway stations. This discount is applied to the basic ticket price but not to supplements for special trains.

Children under three travel free; those three to seven pay half fare.

Comment: Service is efficient on the fast trains between major cities, but Second Class trains, although cheap, can be slow and crowded. Supplements are required on fast trains. The already low fares limit the number of cheap tickets available.

Sweden

Unlimited Mileage Passes

Type of ticket or pass	Valid for	Cost (U.S. dollars)	
		First Class	Second Class
Scandinavian Rail Pass	21 days	$280	$187

See the entry under Denmark in this chapter for complete information on the Scandinavian Rail Pass.

Other Special Tickets and Passes
Children under six travel free; those 6 to 16 pay half fare.

With proof of age, seniors 65 and over receive a 30-percent reduction on all fares (Second Class only).

Two to five persons traveling together constitute a "group"; the first person pays full fare, and the others receive a 30-percent reduction.

Comment: Reservations are mandatory on some trains.

Switzerland

Unlimited Mileage Passes

Type of ticket or pass	Valid for	Cost (U.S. dollars)	
		First Class	Second Class
Swiss Holiday Card	4 days	$120	$ 80
	8 days	140	95
	15 days	165	115
	1 month	235	160

You can buy the Swiss Holiday Card from travel agencies, from the Swiss National Tourist Office in the United States, at major rail stations in Switzerland, and at the Zurich and Geneva airports. It is valid for unlimited travel on the Swiss Federal Railway, plus all boats and postal buses within the country. Holders may also buy reduced-price tickets (20 to 50 percent discounts) for excursions to mountaintops on aerial cableways and cable cars. Children 6 to 16 pay half fare on the Holiday Cards.

Other Special Tickets and Passes

The Half-Fare Travel Card, sold by the Swiss National Tourist offices in New York and San Francisco, allows a 50-percent reduction on all federal trains, post buses, lake steamers, and private trains. It costs $37 for one month or $56 for one year. The Junior Half-Fare Card for those 16 to 26 costs $16 for a month. Holders of Half-Fare Travel Cards can buy "day tickets," each good for a day of unlimited travel while the Half-Fare Card is valid. The "day tickets," which can be purchased only in Switzerland, cost SFr150 (Second Class) and SFr235 (First Class) for six days.

Children under 6 travel free; children 6 to 16 pay half fare.

Comment: Switzerland operates a sliding-fare structure that offers cheaper round-trip than one-way tickets. Examine your planned itinerary carefully to determine whether the Swiss Holiday Card or the Half-Fare Travel Card is the better buy. If you can't take advantage of a special program, remember that a round-trip ticket is up to 20 percent cheaper than two one ways.

Seat reservations cannot be made on internal train services except by groups of ten or more people traveling together.

Ordinary and excursion tickets for local areas can now be purchased conveniently at automatic ticket dispensers on station concourses. These take coins and SFr20 notes, and they give change.

Switzerland has one of the most integrated railway networks in Europe, with more than 3,000 miles of electrified lines. Both Geneva and Zurich airports have their own railway stations.

United Kingdom

Unlimited Mileage Passes

Type of ticket or pass	Valid for	Cost (U.S. dollars) First Class	Second Class
BritRail Pass	8 days	$230	$166
	15 days	350	249
	22 days	440	319
	1 month	520	369

Senior Citizen BritRail	8 days	195	—
	15 days	295	—
	22 days	375	—
	1 month	445	—
Youth BritRail	8 days	—	139
	15 days	—	209
	22 days	—	269
	1 month	—	309
Child BritRail	8 days	139	115
	15 days	209	175
	22 days	269	220
	1 month	309	250

The above rates will be valid from January through December 31, 1988. These passes can be bought only outside Britain. Persons 60 and older qualify for the BritRail Senior Citizen Pass. The Youth Pass is for those 16 to 25; the children's pass is for those 5 to 15.

Other Special Tickets and Passes

"Annual Railcards" are sold only in the United Kingdom for seniors, families, and young persons (formerly designated as students), allowing half-fare travel, with certain restrictions at peak hours. Senior citizens must show senior ID and/or passport. The young-person railcard applies to any person under 24 or anyone who is a student at a British college or university.

"The London Travel Pak," sold only in the United States, includes round-trip rail from Gatwick airport to Victoria Station or round-trip transfers from Heathrow airport to central London by airbus or underground, a London Visitor's Travelcard pass good for three consecutive days of travel on the underground and red buses, and a four-day BritRail Pass for unlimited travel in Britain. Prices in U.S. dollars are noted below.

Economy Class
    Adult
        $149
        $119
    Child (5–15)
        $75
        $70
    Senior Citizen (60 or older)
        $135

Comment: There are no supplements on the InterCity 125 trains, except for seat or sleeper reservations.

Yugoslavia

Unlimited Mileage Passes
None.

Other Special Tickets and Passes
None.

Comment: The country has two major northwest and southeast travel corridors linked laterally by three or four smaller routes. The large eastern cities are served by slow but reliable trains. There is no railway service along the coast. Connections from inland cities to Dubrovnik and other major resort centers are slow.

Train service is very inexpensive in Yugoslavia. However, supplements are charged on all internal express (rapid) trains.

To obtain information on the rail services described in this chapter, please contact the offices listed below.

NATIONAL RAILWAYS

Belgian National Railroad
745 Fifth Avenue
New York, NY 10151
212-758-8130

BritRail
630 Third Avenue
New York, NY 10017
212-599-5400

800 South Hope Street
Suite 603
Los Angeles, CA 90017
213-624-8787

C.I.E. Tours (Irish railways)
122 East 42nd Street
New York, NY 10168-0015
212-972-5600

Eurailpass
610 Fifth Avenue
New York, NY 10020
212-586-0091

French National Railroads (SNCF)
610 Fifth Avenue
New York, NY 10020
212-582-2816

German Federal Railroad
747 Third Avenue, 33rd floor
New York, NY 10017
212-308-3100

Italian State Railways
c/o C.I.T. Travel Service
666 Fifth Avenue, 6th floor
New York, NY 10103
212-397-2667

Netherlands Board of Tourism
355 Lexington Avenue
New York, NY 10017
212-370-7367

Netherlands National Tourist Office
605 Market Street
San Francisco, CA 94102
415-543-6772

Swiss Federal Railways
608 Fifth Avenue
New York, NY 10020
212-757-5944

14

Rental and Lease Cars

Driving can be both an economical and an enjoyable way to get around Europe, as illustrated by the comparisons in chapter 12. Although the enjoyment is not dependent on where you rent, costs are. Car rentals are much more expensive in some countries than others. This cost disparity is due both to differences in basic rates and to differences in the value-added tax (VAT), a surcharge tax imposed by national governments (somewhat like our state sales taxes but usually higher) that can add as much as 25 percent to the price of the rental. Rates among different rental companies can also vary substantially for the same country or region.

LOWEST-COST RENTALS IN EACH COUNTRY

Table 5 (pages 150–151) shows the lowest unrestricted weekly rental costs, including taxes, for a standard subcompact car and for a standard four-door midsize car in 17 European countries (plus Israel) last summer. The cost figure used for each country reflects the rates of the rental company that offered the lowest rates in that country. Add 10 percent to 1987 figures for a reasonable estimate of what you'll pay this summer.

Table 5   1987 Weekly Rental Costs (U.S. dollars, taxes included)

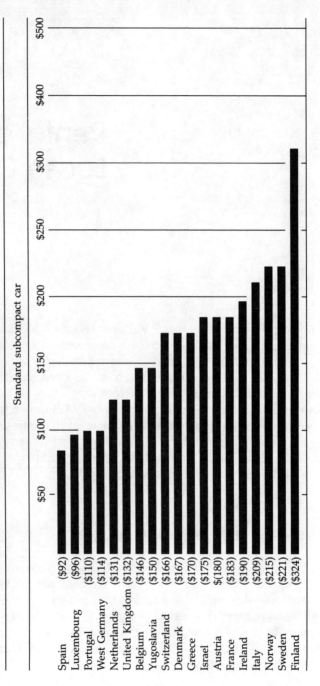

Standard subcompact car

Spain ($92)
Luxembourg ($96)
Portugal ($110)
West Germany ($114)
Netherlands ($131)
United Kingdom ($132)
Belgium ($146)
Yugoslavia ($150)
Switzerland ($166)
Denmark ($167)
Greece ($170)
Israel ($175)
Austria $($180)
France ($183)
Ireland ($190)
Italy ($209)
Norway ($215)
Sweden ($221)
Finland ($324)

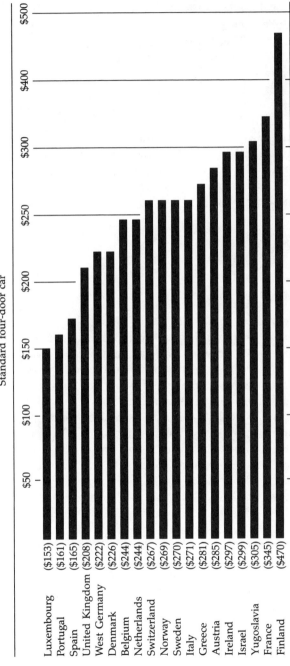

Standard four-door car

The table highlights the range in cost for what is essentially the same product, depending on the country, in which you rent. Although not specifically included in the table, the country-by-country cost pattern for standard subcompact and four-door cars should hold for other sizes and models as well.

The figures used in table 5 apply to special rental programs designed for tourists from the United States. In most cases, they are substantially lower than the rates you would pay if you just walked into a local car-rental office in Europe. Also, these cost figures include applicable VATs. They do not include optional collision-damage waiver coverage (CDW), which reduces the collision deductible to zero, or any other optional insurance coverage sold by the rental companies.

Restrictions

Most unrestricted rental programs offer a high degree of flexibility—about what you'd expect from the major rental companies at home. In most countries you can return cars to different locations within the same country at no additional charge. There are rental offices in most primary and many secondary cities in each country, and at virtually all the international gateway airports. Service is generally available during extended hours, seven days a week, at the bigger city and airport locations. The main qualifications for the tourist rate are that you have to reserve at least 48 hours before you arrive, and you have to rent a car for a minimum of one week.

A few of the rental companies also offer cheaper restricted deals, and offer them in their busiest locations. These restrictions differ among the various rental companies but involve one or more limiting factors:

- advance purchase, similar to APEX airline tickets
- limited rental-office locations, at either major airports or main city-center offices
- pickup and turn in only during normal weekday office hours
- mandatory return to the location where the car was rented

Standard Subcompacts

Almost all European car-rental companies offer one or more of six standard subcompacts in most of their locations: *Fiat Uno, Ford Fiesta, Opel Corsa, Renault 5 le Car, Volkswagen Golf (Rabbit)*, and *Austin Metro*. These cars are usually listed in Group A or Group 1, occasionally in Group O or Group B. Comparable Ford and Volkswagen models are widely sold in the United States and should be familiar to most American motorists; the others are very similar. They're fine city and road cars for two adults and their baggage. They are adequate for two adults plus one child under ten or for two adults plus two very young children. Almost all these models are furnished in two-door or three-door (hatchback) versions. Adults will find it tough getting in and out of the rear seats. Also, neither automatic transmission nor air-conditioning is featured on any of these cars, even as an extra-cost option.

Some companies offer even smaller or older model cars at some locations—for example, *Citroën CV6, Renault 4, Austin Mini, Volkswagen* beetle, and *Fiat Panda*. Of the companies that offer these sub-subcompact cars, some do caution that they are suitable for city driving only.

Insurance

As with U.S. car rentals, the basic European rates include coverage for "third party," fire, and theft claims. They also include collision coverage, with a substantial deductible (as much as the full value of the rented car) for which the renter is liable. This liability can be reduced to zero by a CDW payment, which typically adds about $5 to $10 a day to the rental contract.

Most American drivers' own automobile policies cover rental-car collision damage in the United States and Canada, but not in Europe. You have to buy CDW or accept the financial risk of paying for any damage you sustain.

CDW is a very poor buy when compared with other insurance. But you shouldn't look at it strictly as insurance against accident liability. Instead, view it as insurance against having your trip spoiled or sidetracked by hassles and delays. What you're really paying for is peace of mind.

The special lease programs typically include full zero-deductible collision insurance at no extra cost.

TRADING UP

With three adults—or two adults and two children—you'll probably want a car slightly larger than a standard subcompact, such as a *Fiat Ritmo, Ford Escort, Opel Kadett, Renault 9,* or *Volkswagen Jetta.* Costs for stick-shift models of these cars run anywhere from $20 to $70 higher per week (including taxes) than the standard subcompacts. These cars are usually in Groups B, C, 2, or 3. Car-rental companies often describe them as "suitable for four adults." But many Americans feel pretty crowded driving substantial distances with four adults in these models, because many rental companies furnish them mainly in their two- or three-door versions.

You probably shouldn't consider anything smaller than a car in the next-larger group if your group includes four adults. This group normally includes *Fiat Regata, Ford Sierra, Opel Ascona, Renault 18, Volkswagen Passat,* and the like. Most rental companies categorize them as Group D in most countries, but they can be found from Group C to Group G on occasion. Stick-shift models rent for between $50 and $150 more per week than the standard subcompact Group A models.

Automatic transmissions are about $5 a day extra, but they're not usually offered as options on the standard subcompact models, even at extra cost. You have to go up one size class—to models usually offered as stick-shift options in Group B—to get an automatic. With automatics, these cars are usually priced as Group C. Thus, the least expensive automatic you can get will run at least $50 to $100 a week more than the standard subcompact.

Even in warm countries such as Italy and Spain, air-conditioning is an expensive luxury. The cheapest air-conditioned models in Italy, for example, cost $599 a week last year; the cheapest model in all of Europe cost $349 a week, in Spain.

Of course, you can also go the luxury or sporty route in a European car, so long as you're willing to pay. For example, a *Mercedes 280SE* or *Porsche 944* will run about $500 a week or more. Large parties can rent a *Volkswagen* microbus for something in the range of $400 a week.

Finally, you can rent a recreational vehicle (RV) for camping through Europe. Vehicles suitable for four to six travelers start at about $400 a week in the high season, with extra charges for driving more than 1,750 kilometers (1,090 miles) a week. Off-season rentals are about 40 percent less. Europe is full of well-situated campgrounds, and RV travel has become quite popular. Of course, operating expenses for an RV are at least double those of an efficient compact car, and putting lots of miles on a gas-guzzling RV in Europe can add up to a big expense. For a less expensive camping trip, try tent camping with an efficient compact car instead.

Most rental companies use a letter-group system for classifying the cars in their fleets. Although no official industry-wide standards have been adopted, the standard subcompacts are placed in each rental company's Group A more often than in any other. However, in countries where sub-subcompacts are common, the standard subcompacts are often in a more expensive Group B, and the Group A cars are the sub-subcompacts. If the standard subcompacts are in Group A, the cheaper sub-subcompacts (where available) are called Group O or Group X. Similarly, the standard four-passenger models used for this comparison can be found anywhere from Group C to Group G.

These disparities aren't just the result of different rental company practices either. A single company often lists identical cars differently in different countries. Thus, for example, Avis lists an Opel Corsa as Group B in Luxembourg and Group A in Germany.

Obviously, to be realistic, company-by-company and country-by-country price comparisons have to be among comparable *car models*, not necessarily among the same *letter groups*. It's all too easy for a rental company to engage in group inflation that would mislead you completely if you based your comparison shopping strictly on letter groups.

ONE-WAY RENTALS

Several of the independent rental companies have "Continental One-Way" programs. Weekly costs for these rentals are somewhat higher than most single-country rentals. But no drop-off charge is required so long as you rent and return the car in any combination of up to 25 cities in 14 countries. These rentals are tax-free in all countries except Denmark and France. (If you begin this one-way program in either Denmark or France, you'll have to pay 22- or 33-percent tax.) For rentals longer than one week, the prices drop sharply after the first week.

A few companies offer two one-way deals: one available in most major cities, and another, lower-priced offer limited to just a few of the company's key locations (with limited pickup and drop-off options). Check with rental companies for details.

Avis, Hertz, and National, on the other hand, provide free drop-off between some of the larger European cities as a feature of their regular programs but add drop-off charges for other locations. These rentals are always based on regular rates in the originating country, which—depending on your starting point—may be much lower than the special one-way program rates. Check Avis, Hertz, and National brochures for specifics.

LEASES

For several years, a purchase-repurchase lease has been the best deal for travelers needing a car for longer periods of about three weeks up to six months. These contracts are available in both Belgium and France. You buy a factory-new car on a contract that obligates you to sell it back after you have driven it. The rental company takes care of all the paperwork and financing—you're never really aware that you theoretically own the car rather than hold a lease on it. This deal beats ordinary renting because of some complicated combination of circumstances involving export sales and special markets for slightly used cars.

The one caution is that you're literally driving a new car. You are required to abide by break-in procedures, and you may have to cope with minor new-car mechanical adjustments. You can get service, however, at any dealership that handles the brand of car you've leased, and of course, it's at no additional charge.

The best standard 60-day lease arrangements for 1987 started at about $850 in Belgium and France for standard subcompacts, and about $1,100 for one of the standard four-passenger models. Leases are tax-free and include full zero-deductible insurance.

Pickup and return options are limited unless you're willing to pay quite a bit more.

AIRLINE DEALS

Airlines offer rental-car tie-ins that are sometimes less costly than any separate arrangements. This summer you can expect a variety of such promotions.

As indicated in chapter 9, the best of the deals actually amount to airfare subsidies. Over the last few years, some subsidized rentals have occasionally been offered at $1 a week or even free; more often at $49. That's only for the first week, of course; extra weeks are usually priced at the cooperating rental company's normal rates. These deals are based on a minimum of two people traveling together, who are usually given a standard subcompact car. Singles can enjoy a subcompact for a modest supplement, and larger parties qualify for larger cars. Whenever you're checking on a car-rental promotion, be sure to determine if the price is for the car, regardless of how many use it, or if it is quoted on a per-person basis.

The airline deals called *Fly/Drives* are often very good, provided they can be used with the lowest available airfare. In fact, a good rental-car deal may well be the most important factor in airline selection. But watch out for what look like great deals that require you to buy a much more expensive type of airfare than you'd normally use. One of the heavily publicized deals a few years ago was good only for travelers who used a noncompetitively high weekend fare, rather than the cheaper midweek fare.

RENTAL COMPANIES

Six of the 12 organizations specializing in European rentals are multinational car-rental companies with operating divisions or affiliates in both the United States and Europe. International giants Avis, Budget, and Hertz are very active in the market, with fully competitive rates in many countries. Second-tier multinational operations Ansa (American International) and interRent (Dollar) are also prominent. National in the United States represents Europcar in Europe.

The other six U.S. car-rental companies that specialize in European auto rentals and leases are wholesale tour operators. Cortel and Kemwel are major European tour operators that include aggressive car-rental programs, along with many other travel services. Auto Europe, Connex, Europe by Car, and Foremost Euro-Car specialize in rental cars. In any case, these companies do not have rental operations; they merely package and market the rentals. In fact, on-the-spot service on a rental from one of these operators is often provided by one of the major multinationals.

Finally, some European car dealers in the United States can arrange purchase-repurchase leases for their makes of car. The leases are operated out of Belgium and France, regardless of where the car is manufactured.

The different kinds of companies offer generally competitive rates. To get these rates, you have to reserve in advance. As mentioned, you'll have to pay much more if you just show up at a rental counter. But there are also some important operational differences among the companies.

- The multinational car-rental companies typically allow you either to pay in advance or to pay at the end of your rental, by cash or with a major credit card, whereas the tour operators require full payment in advance.
- Avis, Budget, Europcar (National), and Hertz now require reservations only 48 hours in advance to qualify for the tourist rates; Ansa and interRent require a week. The tour operators have no minimum, but late rentals (within two or three weeks) usually entail extra late charges and special fees for telephone and telex messages.
- Most firms require a minimum one-week rental to qualify for the special tourist rates, but Cortell offers special tourist rates on rentals as short as three days. However, per-day prices for the shorter rentals are quite a bit higher than for weekly rentals.

Pricing

Rental companies' brochures show European rental rates in U.S. dollars only, or in U.S. dollars and local currency. With some, dollar prices are official—they're what you pay no matter what happens to exchange rates. All Connex and Cortell (and some Auto

Europe and Europe by Car) rentals are established officially in U.S. dollars. Of course, these rental companies reserve the right to readjust their rates in the event of a substantial shift in currency-exchange levels.

For others, the official rates are established in the local currencies of individual countries, except in Israel and Yugoslavia, where rentals are expressed by all rental companies in U.S. dollars. (In a few other countries as well, rates are expressed by some rental companies only in U.S. currency.) Dollar figures cited in brochures are "for guidance only," and what you really pay is the dollar equivalent of the foreign-currency rental rate at exchange rates that prevail when you pay—at pickup or drop-off. When comparing rates from different rental companies, you may have to recalculate the dollar cost of any rentals officially priced in local currency to reflect the latest value of the currency.

Note of caution: Several years ago, some car-rental companies either deliberately or inadvertently used very unrealistic exchange rates to calculate those "for guidance only" dollar figures in their rental brochures. Thus, for example, in its first in-depth look at European auto rentals, *Economy Traveler* found companies that used exchange rates that overstated the value of the dollar by as much as 10 percent, thereby understating the actual cost of their rentals by 10 percent. Moreover, the newsletter found that the dollar had never been at the inflated value used to calculate the "guidance" rates at any time during the period when prices were established and brochures printed.

Three years ago, the dollar's steady climb against European currency resulted in overstated dollar figures for the actual rental costs given by companies that quote their official prices in local currency. So no one was hit with an unexpectedly high rental bill because of understated dollar rates.

Now that the dollar is weak, you may again see accidentally or deliberately understated dollar costs from a few companies whose official prices are stated in local currency. Your protection? Read the small print and recalculate any dollar equivalents of local currency.

Austrian rates are based on a VAT reduced from the usual 31 percent to a special tourist rate of 21.3 percent, available on reñtals up to 21 days. If you're renting for 22 days or more, consider renting in Germany.

Tourists who rent cars in Israel (and pay in dollars) are exempt from the usual tax. Make sure your contract shows no tax charge.

Note of caution: If you elect to go with one of the international car-rental chains and you want to pay by credit card when you turn the car in, be sure to pay with a bank card (such as MasterCard or Visa) or a travel and entertainment card (such as American Express or Diners Club) rather than a car-rental-company credit card. In prior years, some car-rental companies have seriously gouged their customers by using unofficial exchange rates well below the actual bank rates prevailing at the time of the charge. It's too early to say how the companies will operate this year, but you're certainly safe with one of the bank cards. They typically give you the official rate on any converted currency billings. Travel and entertainment cards charge a 1 percent exchange fee, but they also give you the official rate.

ADJACENT-COUNTRY RENTING

If you take the lowest-cost unrestricted rental for a standard subcompact car as an overall index of the car-rental costs levels in each European country—a pretty good standard of comparison, by the way—you'll see that car-rental costs in Spain, Luxembourg, Portugal, and West Germany are substantially lower than in some adjacent countries that are important tourist destinations. With rental costs in centrally situated Luxembourg set as a standard, for example, costs in Switzerland are 7 percent higher, costs in Austria are 88 percent higher, and costs in France and Italy are more than twice as high.

This disparity naturally gives rise to the thought that renting a car in one of the low-cost countries, even if you're mainly interested in using it in one of the higher-cost countries, may be the most economical way to go. There's no overall advice to be given here, but two major guidelines can be drawn:

1. If your trip involves driving through both high- and low-cost car-rental countries, it's clearly advantageous to arrange your itinerary to take advantage of the rates in a low-cost country. Your decision to do this is made even easier by the fact that some countries with low-cost rentals also generally enjoy low airfares from the United States. Thus, Barcelona, Düsseldorf, Frankfurt, Luxembourg, and Munich are excellent arrival gateway choices.

2. If you don't really want to spend much time in one of the low-cost countries, the choice is harder. Remember (from chapter 11) that your "overhead" cost of just being in Europe is $125 to $265 a day. So it doesn't pay to spend an extra day or two driving from a low-cost gateway to a high-cost country unless you save at least this amount on car-rental expenses. On the other hand, if your itinerary calls for travel near one of the low-cost gateways, you could save a substantial amount on a car rental (and possibly airfare as well) by using an alternative low-cost gateway.

Adjacent-country renting can be attractive for certain destinations:

- The French VAT, at 33 percent, is equal to the highest in Europe, and total rental costs in France are very high. Unless you're willing to submit to this degree of taxation, consider adjacent-country renting—Frankfurt or Luxembourg if you're heading for northern France, Barcelona for the south. Or use one of the tax-free leases, even for trips as short as three weeks.
- Basic rates are very high in Austria and Switzerland. Munich provides an easy alternative to these countries. Although rates are also high in Finland, Italy, Norway, and Sweden, no nearby countries with low-cost rentals are easily accessible to them.

ARRANGING YOUR RENTAL OR LEASE

With no firm 1988 rates available at press time, you should verify current rental-cost information from several of the lowest-cost suppliers when you're ready to reserve. When you get the brochures, be sure to note which rates are officially established in dollars and which are in local currency. Then recalculate all rates based on local currencies to dollar figures with the latest exchange rates and make your comparisons.

Also, check with the airline you're planning to use—or any others that serve the route you're going to take—to see whether any are offering subsidized rentals in the areas you plan to visit.

If you decide to rent a car yourself, with no airline tie-in, you can arrange your rentals either through your travel agent or directly. If you want one of the purchase-repurchase leases, contact one of the European auto specialists; the major international chains generally don't handle the leases. French and Belgian purchase-repurchase leases may also be offered by one of your local European car dealers.

MAJOR CAR-RENTAL COMPANIES SERVING EUROPE

Ansa International Rent-A-Car (American International): 800-527-0202
Auto Europe: 800-223-5555; 800-237-2465 in ME
Avis Rent-a-Car: 800-331-2112
Budget Rent-a-Car: 800-527-0700
Connex International: 800-445-7404; 800-642-0669 in NY
The Cortell Group: 800-223-6626; 800-442-4481 in NY
Europcar Car Rental System (National): 800-227-7368
Europe by Car: 800-223-1516; 212-581-3040 in NY
Foremost Euro-Car: 800-423-3111; 800-272-3299 in CA
Hertz Rent-a-Car: 800-654-3001
interRent Car Rental System (Dollar): 800-421-6878; 800-457-9040 in CA
The Kemwel Group: 800-468-0468

A few words for the first-time European driver: The idea of driving a rental car in Europe intimidates some Americans, but it's really easier than you might think. Anyone who has driven in Los

Angeles or Boston can cope with most European cities. Highway and destination signs in Europe are probably better than those in many parts of the United States. Most traffic signs use standard graphic symbols that don't depend on language. Traffic rules are also fairly standard—and simple—throughout Europe.

If your main worry is heavy city traffic, remember that a rental car isn't really the best form of transportation for seeing cities. If your trip involves the major capital cities, you're usually better off on the train. Driving is especially suited to the countryside, where traffic problems are minimal, and most American drivers adjust rapidly to local conditions.

The thought of driving on the "wrong" side of the road in the United Kingdom poses special terrors for the uninitiated. Again, however, most drivers find the anticipation worse than the fact. It takes perhaps 10 to 20 minutes and then you begin to feel surprisingly adjusted.

But don't sign up for an expensive long rental if you're really hesitant about driving in Europe. Instead we suggest you take a one- or two-day trial rental. If you're comfortable, extend your rental or plan on extended driving the next time.

When you decide to try a rental car, you'll need your regular state driver's license and a major credit card, just as you do when renting a car in the United States. Check with your car-rental company for full particulars on documentation, especially if any driver in your party is under 21 or over 70.

15

Flying Around Europe

Most official European airfares are high in comparison with domestic U.S. fares for comparable distances. The contrast in fares is even greater since the deregulation of the U.S. airline industry. The officially sanctioned airline cartel agreements in Europe place travel consumers' interests well behind the profitability of the national airlines and the governments' desires to minimize competition from other countries—including the United States.

Until recently, the collaboration between scheduled International Air Transport Association (IATA) airlines and European governments maintained a very rigid official air-travel market. Bucket-shop travel agents that sold discounted airline tickets were considered shady at best, and often operated mainly within ethnic communities.

But that picture has changed radically in the last few years. With increased publicity, various forms of discounted tickets have become more and more popular, for both vacation and business travel. Publications such as *Holiday Which?* and *Business Traveller* in the United Kingdom and *Consumer Reports Travel Letter* in the United States have publicized ticket-discounting practices. American experience with deregulation has not gone unnoticed. European travelers now know that the old IATA cartel arrangement is not the only way an air-transport system can be run. As a result, ticket discounting has become common practice in most European countries, with respectable travel agencies, corporate travelers, and individual vacationers all benefiting. But some governments still believe in the IATA price-fixing doctrines: Discounts below official fares are still hard to find in Austria, France, Italy, Norway, Sweden, Switzerland, and Germany.

Flying is the only viable alternative for some types of trips. As discussed in chapter 12, the fastest surface transportation may be impractical if you want to visit two or three spots in different corners of Europe on a single short trip. To travel from London to Athens by train and channel boat, for example, means leaving on a Monday evening to arrive Thursday afternoon. The somewhat more prosaic train trip from Paris to Naples takes 24 hours; from London to Venice takes 32 hours. And even such short trips as London to Paris or Copenhagen to Stockholm can use up a full day of travel time, largely because of the necessary train-boat-train connections required to get across various channels and straits. If your trip involves intra-European links like these, you should think about flying as a time-saving mode of travel that may justify its higher cost over train or car in the usable touring time you gain.

Fortunately, you're not always stuck with the official fares. European travelers don't like high airfares any better than anyone else, and there are some methods that Europeans use to avoid them that American travelers should use too.

OFFICIAL AIRFARES

How high are regular European airfares? For a simple trip like Frankfurt-Munich-Zurich-Paris-Frankfurt, the fare is about $680. That's about 70¢ a mile. At that rate, you'd pay $137 one way from Boston to New York, or $250 from Los Angeles to San Francisco. Note that these prices were converted from local currencies at August 1987 rates. They should be good for illustrative and comparative purposes. Check for latest prices at the most current conversion rates when planning and budgeting.

As in the United States and across the Atlantic, the airlines within Europe offer the restricted excursion as their best deal for cost-conscious vacation travelers. On some routes, a spectrum of excursion fares is offered, with (typically) comparatively few seats allocated to the very cheapest tickets.

Most of the lowest official fares require a Saturday-night stay. The main exceptions are some of the excursions available on the newly liberalized Netherlands–United Kingdom routes. Some have other restrictions such as advance-purchase requirements. All these fares are intended for round-trips, although you may be able to book open-jaw itineraries for some low fares, providing that both the arrival and departure cities are within one country—for example, fly from London to Nice and return to London from Bordeaux. Late-booking fares are available on a few routes, reservable only within a day or two of departure. You can also get Standby fares on some domestic British services, but not on most other European routes.

Many U.S. travelers would like to use one-way tickets within Europe to fill in the open ends of an open-jaw APEX from the United States to Europe. Unfortunately, you still have to pay dearly for one-way tickets. The lowest official one-way fare is the rather expensive Eurobudget fare. On even the relatively deregulated Netherlands–United Kingdom route, the price reductions have focused mainly on excursion fares, and one-way fares remain expensive. In practice it may be cheaper to buy a round-trip discount or charter ticket and not use the return half.

There are some halting moves afoot to liberalize the entire airline system within the European Economic Community (EEC). Several proposals have been made, but opposition to deregulation is deeply entrenched, and none of the liberalization proposals are likely to do you any good in 1988. It's more likely that the milestone British-Dutch agreement will trigger some comparable agreements between other individual countries.

Meanwhile, if you prefer air travel within Europe as the best alternative for your trip, there is one more option to check: full-fare Economy Class tickets to Europe. Although full fare Economy is a poor buy for point-to-point travel, it allows stopovers at no extra charge within specified generous mileage limitations. Thus you may book a flight from your home city to the most distant city you want to visit in Europe that will provide stopovers at the other cities you want to visit at no additional cost. Your transatlantic airline or travel agent can give you the specific costs for the itinerary you may be planning. But if full-fare Economy looks like a good bet for your trip, check on upgrading to Business Class. On many routes, you would pay only a little more for a much higher standard of quality.

The foregoing comments apply to international fares within

Europe—that is, traveling from country to country. But some of the European countries are big enough that you may be interested in domestic service as well. All European countries of any size have well-established domestic air services, in most cases operated by the national airline. In a few countries, the fares are subsidized at low levels. For example, in Greece a one-way fully flexible Economy fare from Athens to Rhodes (264 miles) costs just $31 at current exchange rates. But in most, fares are at the same high levels as the international fares.

Air Inter, the French domestic air carrier, introduced an unlimited air travel pass valid from April to December 1987. Priced at approximately $225 (FF1,400), it offered unlimited travel on any seven days over a 30-day period. It also provided for a 50-percent discount on specified car rentals and up to a 40-percent discount on selected hotels. Air Inter flies to 30 cities within France, and may prove to be a possible alternative to the France Railpass, an unlimited-mileage rail pass discussed in chapter 13.

Braathens Safe, the domestic air carrier of Norway, offers three special fares during the peak summer season: (1) "Minifare," a special month round-trip fare between all major cities within Norway; (2) "Summer Fare," a flat-rate fare of Nkr 340 for one-way travel in southern Norway; and (3) "Visit Norway Pass," fixed fares for tickets with either four ($195) or eight ($295) flight coupons.

British Airways has instituted a "Highland Rover" in Scotland, permitting eight separate flights during a 14-day period on the Highlands Division network of British Airways, which stretches from the Shetland Isles in the far north to the Hebridean Islands off the west coast, across to Aberdeen in the northeast and Glasgow in the south. The ticket can also be used to fly to the Orkney Islands and Inverness. The ticket must be bought and paid for not less than 14 days before the first flight. It can be used on only one return trip between any two points. The cost is £159 ($254). Last summer, Dan Air launched a "Visit UK" fare costing $66 for the first flight, $99 for two flights, then $49 for each additional flight. Tickets are valid for 30 days; once ticketed, flights can be changed for a fee of $25. Tickets can be bought only in the United States and Canada.

One final note on the scheduled airlines. If high fares are not bad enough, intra-European airline comfort levels are well below those in the United States. Seat pitch is routinely as low as 29 inches, allowing substantially less front-to-rear room than even the lowest-quality U.S. airlines. And on the very popular A300 Airbus

planes, the main workhorse of the heavy traffic routes, some airlines stuff nine seats in each row, compared with the eight seats
that are normal for U.S. operators of the same aircraft.

CHARTER AND INCLUSIVE TOUR FLIGHTS

One of the big differences between civil aviation in the United
States and Europe is the tremendous importance of the charter in
Europe. About a third of all air passengers leaving Britain, Germany, and Scandinavia each year travel on charter flights. These
are mainly vacationers flying off to southern Europe. But there
are also some specialized charter flights on routes linking major
cities.

In general, these charter flights provide the cheapest way to fly
within Europe. Although the "minimal accommodation" requirements (explained below) may sound rather suspicious, this kind of
arrangement is available from all the largest and most respectable
tour operators as well as a multitude of small companies.

International regulations require that between most European
countries, charter seats can be retailed only as part of an "inclusive
tour" holiday that includes some "land package" arrangement such
as a hotel room or rental car. But most European tour operators sell
at least some of their charter seats with only the barest minimum
accommodation to satisfy the letter if not the spirit of the regulation, for example, a bed in a dormitory of accommodations in a
hostel that might not even exist. The traveler therefore pays only
slightly more than the price of the air ticket, and this price is often
well below the cheapest fare on the scheduled flights.

The prices of seats on charter flights are not government-con-
trolled, and the market works very much according to supply and
demand. Prices rise steeply at peak periods on the "sunshine"
routes to the Mediterranean. They may also be cut dramatically if a
tour operator is left with unsold seats shortly before flight date.

The European charter business is so big that the major airlines
regularly sell blocks of seats on their scheduled flights to tour operators. Once again, regulations state that these seats can be sold only
as part of a package holiday that includes accommodations. But
these rules are widely ignored by tour operators, with the full
knowledge of the airlines. These fares are known as "inclusive
tour" fares, or consolidations. Tour operators who specialize in

selling this type of "package" are generally known as consolidators.

Charter flights do have some disadvantages. They are generally even less comfortable than scheduled flights, with less legroom and fairly basic in-flight catering. Tickets are normally available only for round-trip travel: One-way fares are occasionally offered but usually cost 70 to 80 percent of the round-trip fare. Many routes are served by only one flight each way, each week. And charter operators sometimes alter schedules by as much as a full day shortly before departure. Don't rely on a charter to make a close connection with a transatlantic flight.

However, on a few main routes there are charter operators with daily or almost-daily flights that allow you to choose any length of stay. From London, Pegasus Skybus and Pilgrim Air offer this kind of quasi-scheduled service to Italy; GTF Tours offers it to Austria, Germany, and Switzerland; and City by City provides services to Switzerland. Falcon and Slade also offer quasi-scheduled services to a wide selection of European destinations.

For a wider choice of flight dates at slightly higher prices, it is worth looking at the inclusive tour deals on scheduled flights— sold on the same minimal-accommodation basis as the charters. They are also available only as round-trips (no open-jaw travel); most require that you stay a Saturday night at your destination. However, they do not have any advance booking restrictions, so they are particularly useful on routes like those from London to Scandinavia or Italy, where the lowest official fares on scheduled flights are APEX-type fares that must be booked three or four weeks in advance. The two best-known companies selling such tickets from London to many European destinations are Falcon and Slade. There are also companies that specialize in selling tickets for one area: Citalia for Italy, or Scantours and Nordic Fare Deals for Scandinavia, for example.

DISCOUNT FARES

Just about any discussion of European airfares ultimately turns to bucket shops and discount tickets. Unfortunately, if you are planning flights only within Europe, they won't help you much. Such tickets are rarely available for intra-European services. Discount tickets are more frequently available on long-haul routes to the Middle East, Africa, Asia, Australia, and South America. However, several Asian, African, and Middle Eastern airlines operate flights that stop at more than one point in western Europe to add traffic, and some of them discount these intra-European segments.

Discounting comes about because most airlines have more seats than they can sell at the officially agreed high prices. So they sell them off unofficially at much-reduced rates. Discounting is against the rules of IATA, but it is certainly not illegal for customers to buy such tickets. Several European governments, notably the British and Dutch, believing that many of the official fares are much too high, have consistently turned a blind eye to discounting. The Germans, on the other hand, sporadically attempt to "clean up" the airline-ticket marketplace—to no ultimate avail, but to the short-term consternation of airlines and travel agents.

BUYING YOUR TICKETS

If you're interested mainly in excursion tickets on the scheduled airlines, you can buy them from your regular travel agent, at home, at the same price that you would pay in Europe. As a result of attorney Don Pevsner's 1978 action, airlines can no longer prevent U.S. travel agents from selling even the cheapest intra-European tickets. The price you pay is simply the going price in the country where the trip originates, as expressed in local currency, converted to U.S. dollars on the day you buy the ticket. Of course, you can wait until you get to Europe to buy. You don't have to, however, and you may not be able to, depending on restrictions that may apply to the fare you are prepared to pay.

You do have to wait to get to Europe to buy charter and discount tickets. Until quite recently, these tickets were sold mainly by bucket shops. These agencies, usually in central-city areas, were partially outside the system and weren't fully accredited by the organizations that accredit European travel agencies. But recently more and more respectable, fully accredited travel agents have started selling discount tickets quite openly. The large travel-agency chains now sell discount tickets in all their retail shops. The small bucket shops are still very much in business, though. They operate primarily by placing small ads in the classified columns of newspapers and magazines.

It's often suggested, especially by IATA apologists, that buying discount tickets is courting disaster: The agent will disappear with your money or the airline won't honor the ticket or some other catastrophe will occur. *Holiday Which?*, the British consumer travel magazine, suggests that these fears are much exaggerated. A survey carried out during the summer of 1984 indicated that although the incidence of minor problems is quite high—particularly ticket delivery later than expected—major problems were not common. However, anyone planning to buy a discount ticket should take some sensible precautions:

- Get full details of takeoff and landing times, plane changes, and so on. For scheduled flights you can check the details with the airline itself.
- Get full details about your tickets: Are there minimum- and maximum-stay requirements? Can you alter your flight dates after booking? What refund can you expect if you cancel?
- Find out whether the travel agent is fully accredited. If not, be wary of paying more than a small deposit before tickets are delivered.

You may well find that you don't have enough time after your arrival in Europe to make the necessary arrangements. Bucket-shop ticket purchases are seldom as quick as purchases from an airline or a conventional travel agent. The only easy answer to this problem is to have friends or acquaintances who live in Europe buy the tickets for you. However, that suggestion doesn't help the vast majority of Americans who do not have such European friends or relatives. A few U.S. agents that sell discounted transatlantic tickets may be able to obtain intra-European tickets, given sufficient lead time. It's worth asking, if you're dealing with a discount ticket agent here. And of course, Americans can write to British or Dutch agents that advertise in publications available here. But frankly, none of the alternatives measures up to the standards of convenience and reliability that would warrant an endorsement in this book.

Don't try to buy unofficial tickets at an airline office—even on that particular airline. An airline will offer you only the officially approved fares; it will not tell you about any cheap package deals (even on its own flights) or any other forms of discount travel.

AIRFARE EXAMPLES

Here is a sampling of summer season 1987 intra-European air-fares—official, charter, and discount. Fares are quoted from London and Amsterdam, probably Europe's two most competitive air-travel markets.

The cheapest available one-way tickets are typically Eurobudget fares. They have no advance-purchase restrictions, but the number of Eurobudget seats allocated to each flight may be small. The lowest excursion fares available on scheduled airlines (APEX, PXE, and Latesaver) typically have restrictions, including some combination of advance purchase, Saturday-night stay, and unlimited availability.

Charter/discount tickets typically have fewer or no restrictions, but many of them are available only on connecting flights or flights that make one or more stops. For example, the lowest available fare from Amsterdam to Athens is on Interflug (the East German airline), with a connection in East Berlin.

All scheduled-airline fares were quoted in pounds sterling by British Airways (London) and/or in guilders (florin) by KLM (Amsterdam) and converted to U.S. dollars at late 1987 rates.

London–Amsterdam
Official airline fares
    Lowest unrestricted
Economy (one way): $118
    Lowest excursion (round-trip): $112
    Latesaver round-trip: $63
Typical 1987 charter/discount fare
    Round-trip: $96

London–Frankfurt
Official airline fares
    Lowest unrestricted
Economy (one way): $181
    Lowest excursion (round-trip): $136
Typical 1987 charter/discount fare
    Round-trip: $122

London–Paris
Official airline fares
    Lowest unrestricted
Economy (one way): $131
    Lowest excursion (round-trip): $133
Typical 1987 charter/discount fare
    Round-trip: $105

London–Rome
Official airline fares
    Lowest unrestricted
Economy (one way): $288
    Lowest excursion (round-trip): $249
Typical 1987 charter/discount fare
    Round-trip: $175

London–Athens
Official airline fares
    Lowest unrestricted
Economy (one way): $358
    Lowest excursion (round-trip): $314
    Latesaver round-trip: $157
Typical 1987 discount fare
    Round-trip: $96

London–Tel Aviv
Official airline fares
    Lowest unrestricted
Economy (one way): $748
    Lowest excursion (round-trip): $841
Typical 1987 charter/discount fare
    Round-trip: $290

London–Cairo
Official airline fares
    Lowest unrestricted
Economy (one way): $549
    Lowest excursion (round-trip): $740
Typical 1987 charter/discount fare
    Round-trip: $389

Amsterdam–Rome
Official airline fares
    Lowest unrestricted
Economy (one way): $433
    Lowest excursion (round-trip): $252
Typical 1987 charter/discount fare
    Round-trip: $123

Amsterdam–Madrid
Official airline fares
    Lowest unrestricted
Economy (one way): $440
    Lowest excursion (round-trip): $320
Typical 1987 charter/discount fare
    Round-trip: $134

Amsterdam–Stockholm
Official airline fares
    Lowest unrestricted
Economy (one way): $434
    Lowest excursion (round-trip): $394
Typical 1987 charter/discount fare
    Round-trip: $163

Amsterdam–Athens
Official airline fares
    Lowest unrestricted
Economy (one way): $610
    Lowest excursion (round-trip): $293
Typical 1987 charter/discount fare
    Round-trip: $163

Amsterdam–Tel Aviv
Official airline fares
    Lowest unrestricted
Economy (one way): $861
    Lowest excursion (round-trip): $480
Typical 1987 charter/discount fare
    Round-trip: $235

This sampling should illustrate two important points about flying within Europe:

1. There is no real consistency in the relationships among the lowest unrestricted one-way fares, the lowest excursion fares on scheduled airlines, and the cheapest discount tickets.
2. In many instances, the least expensive scheduled-airline excursion is less than half the cost of going one way, so you can save on one-way travel by buying an excursion even if you do not use the return.

Finally, those lowest available Eurobudget (one-way) and excursion (round-trip) fares on the scheduled airlines sell out very quickly during peak travel periods. If you think you're interested, make sure that you reserve as early as possible, preferably at the time you reserve your transatlantic flights. Waiting until you get to Europe could mean you would have to pay a much higher fare.

To obtain information on the services described in this chapter, please contact the companies below.

DISCOUNT LONDON AGENCIES

Citalia Ltd.
50/51 Conduit Street
London WIR 9FB
Telex: 263962

City by City
4 Mays Court
London WC2N 4BS
Telex: 296186

Falcon Leisure Group
Notting Hill Gate
London W11 3JQ
Telex: 883256

GTF Tours, Ltd.
(German Tourist Facilities)
184 Kensington Church Street
Notting Hill Gate, London
W8 4DP
Telex: 263696

Pegasus (Skybus) Holidays
24A Earls Court Garden
London SW5 OTA
Telex: 8952011

Scantours
(Scanbreak/Escape Holidays)
8 Spring Gardens
London SW1A 2BG
Telex: 919008

Slade Travel, Ltd.
15 Vivian Avenue
London NW4 3UT
Telex: 23425

Pilgrim Air
44 Goodge Street
London W1P 1FP
Telex: 267752

Nordic Fare Deals
Norwegian State Railways
   Travel
Norway House
21/24 Cockspur Street
London SW1Y 5DA
Telex: 28380

16

Urban
Transportation

Your final transportation question may seem the simplest, but it may well determine how well you spend your time in Europe. Whether you plan to visit just one city or hope to visit a different one every day, the question remains: What's the best way to travel among hotel, restaurants, and the sights you want to see? The answers naturally lead to a review of buses, streetcars, subways, and taxis in Europe's major cities.

Of course, one way to get around is to rely on organized sightseeing tours. They virtually guarantee that you'll see at least those attractions that conventional wisdom decrees you should see, without any real mental or physical effort on your part. You pay for this security not only with more money—sightseeing excursions are among the most expensive ways of touring a city—but also with a loss of flexibility and independence. Nevertheless, tours are a viable option, especially the lower-cost tours run by the local public-transit systems in many major cities. If nothing else, such tours are a good way to familiarize yourself with a new city that you can later explore on your own.

The other end of the transportation spectrum is walking. Don't sell it short. Americans are so used to jumping into cars to go only a block or two that we sometimes forget how easy it is to see a place by walking through it. Most European city streets were laid out long before anyone ever thought of automobiles, and despite some heroic engineering accomplishments in roads and parking, an automobile can be more of a liability than a convenience in the historic city centers. Even if you're touring by rented car, you may find it easier and cheaper to leave your car parked and get around the city on foot.

If you want to see as much as you can in a limited time, consider a do-it-yourself taxi tour. Find a driver with reasonably good English (if you don't speak the country's language) and tell the driver what you want to see. Taxis in most of Europe are considerably less expensive than U.S. taxis. In fact, two people usually see more in less time, and at less cost, by sharing a taxi than by buying two tickets on a commercial tour bus.

But walking, tour buses, and taxi tours are not really a complete intracity transportation solution for most travelers. Many of the things you want to see are too distant to walk to, and the cost of all-day taxis and tours can add up to more than many want to pay. So you'll get around the city the way most Europeans do: on their generally excellent local and regional transit systems.

The information in this chapter should be used for trip planning and budgeting. No guidebook of this type can substitute for the detailed fare data, schedule information, and system maps that travelers should acquire as soon as they arrive in each new city. For example, although only regular adult transit fares and special tickets designed for tourists are cited here, many of the systems offer special reductions for children and seniors. These and other details should be checked on arrival.

Public-transportation charges are quoted in local currency only. Whatever happens to exchange rates, these fares and ticket costs will remain reasonably stable in local value. Besides, if you're going to be riding around with the locals, you might as well start thinking in terms of the local money. Although no general increase in transportation prices is forecast, rates could still rise about 10 percent in 1988.

Obviously, we can't begin to describe the intricacies of transportation in Europe's major cities—even local residents don't always understand the complexities of some of these systems. So we concentrate on two kinds of information: (1) how to get downtown from the airport(s) and (2) the public transit passes especially designed for travelers. Note that such passes are meant for people who are going to use public transit as their principal means of transportation. They're not for people who hardly venture out of their hotel rooms or who take cabs most places.

The passes aren't always the cheapest way to get around for a few days in a European city, but they're the most hassle-free. You don't have to fumble for change, find out where you can buy a ticket, determine whether you have to validate a ticket, find out how to transfer, and undergo the numerous other minor problems of paying for public transit. You just show your pass and go on your way. We recommend them.

In the following city listings, all times and prices are approximate; the figures in parentheses after the airport name indicate the distance from downtown. (Remember, a kilometer equals .62 miles.) Most public transit to airports operates from around 6:00 A.M. to around 9:00 P.M.

Amsterdam

Airport transportation
Schiphol Airport (15 km)

Taxi: 45 minutes; Df35; no luggage charge

Limousine: KLM Coach bus to Center Station; 35 minutes; F10

Rail: Intercity train (Schiphol Line); 17 minutes; Df2.80

Public transit: B Centraal Nederland bus to Central Station; 35 minutes; Df6.50

Taxi service
You can get cabs at stands or phone 777777. Basic charge, Df3.80 pickup, Df2.23 per km; rates higher at night; no charge for baggage. Amsterdam cabs take four persons maximum per cab.

Public transit
Basic fare: A zone fare system. For streetcars, buses, metro: Df1.75, two-strip ticket; Df2.60, three-strip ticket; Df8.65, ten-strip ticket; available at Central Railway Station, public transport outlets, post offices, and some VVV tourist offices.

Passes for travelers: Good on buses, streetcars, and metro: Df8.65. Day in Amsterdam ticket good for unlimited use one day. Ranger ticket, Df8.65, one day; Df11.60, two days; Df14.20, three days; Df16.90, four days; each extra day, Df2.70, for maximum of nine days.

Athens

Airport transportation

Hellinikon Airport (14 km)

    West airport (Olympic Airways)

    Taxi: 35 minutes; Dr500–Dr875; Dr25 per bag; double fare at night

    Public transit: Bus #133 or #122

    East airport

    Taxi: Same as above

    Public transit: Bus #18 or #121, Dr40

Taxi service

Cabs available on streets and at several central points. Dr25 pickup, Dr26 per km; higher charge outside central area; surcharge for railway station or port pickup, baggage, Dr240-per-hour waiting charge. Minimum fare Dr130. Double fare 1:00–5:00 A.M.

Public transit

Basic Fare: Dr30 for bus and trolley bus and Dr30 for Piraeus metro to Kifissia

Barcelona

Airport transportation

Barcelona Airport (10 km)

    Taxi: 20 minutes; Pts1,500–Pts1,800

    Train: RENFE express train to Sants station; 11 minutes; Pts138

    Public transit: EA local bus to Plaza España; 30 minutes; Pts69; Many stops; no baggage space; connections for metro

Taxi service

Pts200 pickup, Pts70 per km; rates higher at night and in suburbs; extra charge for baggage, bullfight trips, Pts960 per hour waiting time. *Gran tourismo* cabs are higher, with negotiable rates.

Public transit

Basic fare: Pts50 bus; Pts45 metro; Pts50 metro on holidays. Microbus is slightly higher than bus.

    Passes for travelers: Pts275 for ten-ride book, good for metro, streetcar, and Montjuic funicular

Berlin

Airport transportation

Tegel Airport (7 km)

Taxi: 20 minutes; DM15–DM20; DM1 per bag

Public transit: #9 bus, 35 minutes; DM2.20; space for baggage

Taxi service: You can get cabs at stands and on street; DM3.40 pickup, DM1.60 per km; higher rates at night.

Public transit

Basic fare: DM2.30 bus or metro in city center. Transfers are free on all bus routes, on U-Bahn, and on some S-Bahn suburban services. Twenty-four-hour ticket, DM8, validated by date rather than hour; buy in morning for efficient use.

Passes for travelers: Special tickets for unlimited bus and metro use: DM16, two days; DM32, four days. Buy at Kleistpark metro station or at zoo.

Brussels

Airport transportation

Brussels National Airport (12 km)

Taxi: 20–30 minutes; BF700–BF950

Public transit: Train to Gare du Nord and Gare Centrale; 20 minutes; BF65, Second Class; BF95, First Class; ample baggage space

Taxi service

Cabs are available from designated taxi ranks. BF55 pickup, BF26.50 per km in town, BF54 in suburbs.

Public transit

Basic fare: BF35 single ticket; BF210, ten-trip card; free transfers

Passes for travelers: BF140 unlimited-travel tourist ticket for 24 hours on metro, trams, and buses

Copenhagen

Airport transportation

Kastrup Airport (10 km)

Taxi: 20 minutes; DKr120

Limousine: SAS bus to Central station; 30 minutes; DKr20.

Public transit: Bus #32 local to Town Hall Square; 45 minutes; DKr10; many stops, poor baggage space

Taxi service
Cabs are available on street. DKr15 pickup, DKr7.15 per km. You can also call 1-35-35-35 for cab.

Public transit
Basic fare: DKr6, buses and S-train tickets and discount cards good for one hour within defined zones; DKr12 maximum fare with two-hour limit. Ten-ticket cards available on buses or at train stations.

Passes for travelers: Copenhagen Card tourist ticket: DKr70, one day; DKr130, two days; DKr150, three days

Dublin

Airport transportation
Dublin Airport (6 mi.):
Taxi: 30 minutes; IRL15, plus IRL1.85 pickup
Limousine: CIE airport bus: 45 minutes; IRL3.10
Public transit: Bus #41 to Quay; 1 hour; IRL 80

Taxi service
IRL1.05 pickup, IRL .75 per mi. or 9 minutes; IRL1.80 minimum fare; IRL.40 per additional passenger, IRL .40 per bag, IRL .40 surcharge at night, surcharges for holidays

Public transit
Basic fare: Fares based on stages; one to three stages, IRL .45; four to seven stages, IRL .55. Board bus, wait for fare collector to ask where you're going and to tell you fare. Exact change not required. One-day pass, IRL2.70.

Edinburgh

Taxi service
£.70 pickup, £.40 per km, £.30 surcharge at night; taxi stands at St. Andrews Square Bus Station and Waverley Street Station

Public transit
Basic fare: Stage fares at minimum £.20, maximum £.90; limited stop bus, £.45

Passes for travelers: Tourist Card: one day, £6.95; two days, £8.20; three days, £9.45; four days, £10.70; sold in increments up to 13 days; also provides discounts to some attractions

Florence

Taxi service
There are taxi stands in main piazzas; you can also hail cabs on street; L4,000 pickup, L592 per km; L2,500 surcharge at night, L500 per bag. Surcharges for holidays.

Public transit
Basic fare: L600; eight tickets, L4,200. You have to buy your ticket, before you board bus, at tobacco shops, newspaper stands, or bus-ticket kiosks. Validate ticket in machine on bus.

Passes for travelers: None

Frankfurt

Airport transportation
Frankfurt-Main Airport (12 km)

Taxi: 50 minutes; DM30

Rail: S14 or S15 to downtown Frankfurt; 35 minutes; DM3.10; DM4.40 in rush hours

Public transit: Bus #61 to downtown Frankfurt, 50 minutes; DM3.10; DM4.40 in rush hours

Taxi service
DM3.60 pickup, DM1.80 per km. Cabs can be hailed in street or ordered by phone from 230001, 25001, 230033, or 545011.

Public transit
Basic fare: S-bahn, U-bahn metro, and buses: Zone 1 DM1.50, DM2.20 in rush hours; Zone 1, DM7 for 24-hour pass

Passes for travelers: Eurailpass is valid on S-bahn

Geneva

Airport transportation
Cointrin Airport (4 km)
Taxi: 15 minutes; SF20
Train: SF5 First Class, SF3.50 Second Class

Taxi service
SF5 pickup, SF2 per km; surcharges for night, waiting

Public transit
Basic fare: Three stops in 1 hour, SF1.20; 2 hours, SF2.40; ten-day unlimited travel, SF30. Buy from machines at boarding point or at transportation kiosk in Cornavin Station shopping center

Helsinki

Airport transportation
Helsinki Vantaa Airport (19 km)
Taxi: 20–45 minutes; Mk100
Limousine: 30–45 minutes; Mk12 (to Hotel Inter-Continental)
Public transit: Bus #614 (#616 weekday mornings); 30–45 minutes; Mk9.

Taxi service
Mk10.20 pickup, Mk3.53 per km for two persons, Mk4.25 for three or four persons; Mk4.50 surcharge for nights and weekends

Public transit
Basic fare: Mk6; ten-ride strip, Mk49
Passes for travelers: Helsinki Card, one-day, Mk55; two-day, 75; three-day, Mk45; allows unlimited use of transit, free bus sightseeing tour, admission to some museums, and other benefits

Lisbon

Airport transportation
Portela Airport (8 km)
Taxi: 20 minutes; Esc500, plus Esc50 per piece of luggage or 50-percent surcharge on fare for baggage
Public transit: Green Line bus, 40 minutes; Esc150; little room for baggage

Taxi service

Cabs, which can be hailed or picked up at stands, are metered and inexpensive; Esc70 pickup, Esc31 per km; 20% extra at night. For trips outside city, you pay rate per km to your destination plus charge for return trip, whether you take it or not.

Public transit

Basic fare: Buses and streetcars operate on zone fares, Esc30 for one zone; reduction for ten- or twenty-book tickets; subway, Esc37.50; ten-ticket book, Esc300

Passes for travelers: A tourist pass good for either four days (Esc800) or seven days (Esc1,100) allows travel on all municipal transit; buy at booths marked *Carris* in transit stations from 8:00 A.M.–8:00 P.M.

London

Airport transportation

Heathrow (15 mi.)

Taxi: 45–60 minutes; £20–£22

Limousine: London Transport's Airbus: A1 to Victoria Station and A2 to Euston station, both calling at major hotel areas along route; 50–60 minutes; £3

Public transit: Two Underground stations (Piccadilly Line) serve Heathrow: one for Terminals 1, 2, and 3; the other for Terminal 4; 50 minutes; £1.60; some space for baggage

Gatwick (29 mi.)

Taxi: 45–90 minutes; £27

Train: 30–45 minutes; £4.20 to Victoria Station

Taxi service

80 pence for first 924 yards; 20 pence for each additional 462 yards.

Public transit

Basic fare: Minimum fare on bus in 1987 was 35 pence; on underground, 50 pence. Fares rise with distance traveled. Most visitors use Underground.

Passes for travelers: Visitor Travelcard is easiest and most convenient way to travel around London. Buy in advance from BritRail or some travel agents. Advance-purchase cards are good for three, four, or seven days. These cards aren't available in London. You can buy the seven-day Travelcard in London; photocard costing about £1 required with seven-day pass. Buy at Underground stations and travel-information centers. Phone 222-1234 for information on London Transport.

Luxembourg

Airport transportation
Luxembourg Airport (6 km)
Taxi: 20 minutes; F500, plus F20 for more than 2 bags
Limousine: Luxair bus, 20 minutes; F120
Public transit: Bus "Luxembourg Ville," 20 minutes; F50, including one bag

Taxi service
F19 per km; surcharge of 10% at night

Public transit
Basic fare: F25
Passes for travelers: None

Madrid

Airport transportation
Barajas Airport (16 km)
Taxi: 30 minutes; Pts2,500
Limousine: 30–45 minutes; Pts300

Taxi service
Pts80 pickup, Pts38 per km; Pts975 per hour for waiting

Public transit
Basic fare: Buses: Pts50, Pts60 express bus, Pts310 for ten-ride book. More comfortable Microbus charges Pts60. Subway: Pts50; Pts410 for ten-ride book.
Passes for travelers: None

Milan

Airport transportation
Malpensa Airport (28 km)

Taxi: 1 hour; L40,000–L50,000. Take metered cab; avoid unmetered "gypsy" cabs

Limousine: 1 hour, L6000

Public transit: Bus #73 to center near Duomo; avoid unless you're on a bare-bones budget; no place for luggage and usually very crowded.

Linate Airport (7 km)

Taxi: 20 minutes, L10,000–L20,000

Limousine: 25 minutes; L2500

Taxi service

L4,000 pickup, L800 per km; L2,800 surcharge at night, L500 per bag, L1,000 per km surcharge Sunday and holidays. You can hail cab, but getting one at taxi stand is much easier.

Public transit

Basic fare: L700 for 75 minutes of unlimited travel. Tickets sold at newsstands, tobacco shops, and special kiosks. Validate ticket in machine on bus. Bus and subway tickets not interchangeable.

Munich

Airport transportation

Munich-Riem Airport (10 km)

Taxi: 30 minutes; DM25

Limousine: Munich Airport bus to Hauptbahnhof (central station), 45 minutes, DM5

Taxi service

DM2.90 pickup, DM1.70 per km, DM.50 per bag

Public transit

Basic fare: DM2.30; twenty-four-hour ticket, DM6.50

Passes for travelers: None

Oslo

Airport transportation

Fornebu Airport (10 km)

Taxi: 25 minutes; Kr75; higher at night

Limousine: SAS bus; 25 minutes; Kr20

Public transit: Bus #31; Kr10; many stops into city; no baggage space

Taxi service

You can phone for cab (38-80-90), get one at stand, or hail one on street; Kr13 pickup, 3.5 per km; extra charge at night and for baggage.

Public transit

Basic fare: Kr10, for bus, streetcar, subway, suburban commuter trains, ferries

Passes for travelers: Oslo Card for one day, Kr70; two days, Kr100; three days, Kr130 for unlimited transportation within city; also provides free admission to many museums, discounts on restaurants, sightseeing tours, and the like. Buy at Tourist Information Center (City Hall), at many hotels, and at accommodation center in railway station.

Paris

Airport transportation

Charles de Gaulle Airport (23 km)

Taxi: 45 minutes; FF200–FF250, FF4 per bag

Limousine: Air France bus to Porte Maillot; 45 minutes; F36

Rail: From de Gaulle, take free shuttle bus to Roissy Rail, then train to Gare du Nord; 35 minutes; FF35, First Class; FF23, Second Class. Eurailpass accepted.

Public transit: RATP #350 to Gare de l'Est; #351 to Place de la Nation; 1 hour; FF27.60 or six Metro tickets. Many stops, poor baggage space; an advantage is that you can use *Sésame* pass, if you've purchased one before leaving United States.

Orly Airport (14 km)

Taxi: 35 minutes; FF160–FF200

Limousine: Air France bus to Invalides; 40 minutes; F28

Rail: Take shuttle bus to Orly Rail to Pont St.-Michel station. FF26, First Class; FF17.50, Second Class; Eurailpass accepted.

Public transit: RATP bus #215 to Denfert Rochereau; #183 to Choisy; 40 minutes; FF16.50 (three Metro tickets)

Taxi service

You can get cab at stands, at main intersections, at railway stations, and on street. If you phone for cab, meter starts running when cab is dispatched. FF9 pickup, FF2.44 per km; rates higher at night and in outlying areas; extra charge for railway-station pickup, baggage. Most Paris cabs take only three persons; those that take more require supplement of FF5 per additional person.

Public transit

Basic fare: FF4.70, Second Class; FF6.8, First Class. Metro has both classes; use Second Class tickets on buses. Carnet of 10 tickets in First Class is FF42; in Second Class, FF28.20.

Passes for travelers: Sésame, for unlimited travel on Metro (First Class) and buses, FF57, two days; FF85, four days; FF141, seven days. You can buy at larger Metro stations in Paris. You can also buy one before you leave home: Send check for $9 for two-day pass, $13.50 for four-day pass, or $22 for seven-day pass to Marketing Challenges International, 10 East 21st Street, New York, NY 10010. Allow two weeks for delivery.

Reykjavik

Airport transportation

Keflavik Airport (50 km)

  Taxi: 45 minutes; Kr2,000 days, Kr3,000 nights and weekends
  Limousine: Bus meets every flight; 45–50 minutes, Kr800–Kr900.
  Public transit: Kr170

Taxi service

Kr18 per km

Public transit

Basic fare: Kr28; Kr200 for seven-ticket book
  Passes for travelers: Omnibus Passport for unlimited travel in Iceland, Kr5,800.

Rome

Airport transportation

Fiumicino Airport (Leonardo da Vinci) (32 km)

Taxi: 45–60 minutes; L40,000 (meter reading plus L10,000–L14,000). Make sure you get a metered cab with a working meter.

Limousine: 55–60 minutes; L5,000 to Termini, central station. Watch out for "gypsy" cabs where limousine lets you off at Termini. Be sure you get a metered cab.

Public transit: Not practical, but a direct line is under construction. Check for service.

Taxi service
L2,600 pickup, L266 per minute or 300 meters; L3,000 night surcharge, L500 per bag. You can hail cab, but getting one at taxi stand is much easier.

Public transit
Basic fare: L700 on both buses and Metro, but tickets are not interchangeable; L1,200, 12-hour ticket (2:00 P.M.–midnight); L2,800, 24-hour ticket. Not many visitor attractions are served by Metro; buses are more useful. You have to buy ticket, before you board bus, at tobacco shops, newspaper stands, or bus-ticket kiosks. Validate ticket in machine on bus. Buses are often extremely crowded. Buy Metro tickets from machines in Metro stations.

Passes for travelers: Eight-day tourist bus pass, L10,000. Buy at bus station in front of Termini, central station.

Stockholm

Airport transportation
Arlanda Airport (42 km)
> *Taxi:* 40 minutes; Kr200
> *Limousine:* SAS Limo, 40 minutes, Kr165–Kr210
> *Public transit:* Stockholm Transport, 40 minutes, Kr28

Taxi service
Kr3 per km during day, Kr5 per km at night

Public transit
Basic fare: Kr8; 10-trip ticket, Kr40. Buy at newsstands marked Pressbyra.

Passes for travelers: Stockholm Card, which provides unlimited use of public transit and admission to numerous attractions, costs Kr68 for one day, Kr116 for two days, Kr174 for three days, 232 for four days. The Tourist Card covers public transit and a few attractions: 24 hours for central Stockholm, Kr19; 24 hours for Stockholm and suburbs, Kr33; 72 hours, Kr65.

Venice

Taxi service
Minimum fare for water taxis, L35,000; stiff surcharges apply for nights, bags, waiting time.

Public transit
Basic fare: *Vaporetti*, Venice's canal boats, charge L2,000 for most trips, depending on distance. *Motoscafi*, which ply side canals, charge about the same. *NOTE:* Gondolas are expensive tourist traps.

Passes for travelers: Day ticket, L10,000, available from ticket booths near boat stops

Vienna

Airport transportation
Schwechat Airport (16 km)
   Taxi: 30 minutes; S550
   Limousine: 35 minutes, S60 to Hilton

Taxi service
Minimum fare, S25; get cab at stands or order by phone

Public transit
Basic fare: Bus, streetcar, subway, S19; five-ride book, S65
Passes for travelers: Three Days in Vienna, S83 for unlimited travel. Buy at Vienna Public Transport information offices, advance sales offices, railway stations, and tourist-information offices.

Zurich

Airport transportation
Zurich Airport (Kloten) (12 km)
   Taxi: 15–20 minutes; SF35–SF40
   Train: 10 minutes, SF6.60 First Class, F4.20 Second Class

Taxi service
DSF5.00 pickup, SF2.20 per km

Public transit
Basic fare: Zone fares for one to five stops, SF1; more than five stops, SF1.60; 24-hour ticket, SF5; 12-ticket book for one to five stops, SF10; 12-ticket book for more than 5 stops, SF16. Buy tickets from machines at streetcar and bus stops.

Index

Add-on travel services, 9, 67–68
Ads, *see* Classified ads
Advance-purchase excursion fares, *see* APEX airfares
Advance-purchase requirements;
for airline tickets, 10, 29, 55, 166, 172
for car rentals, 152
Aer Lingus, 27
Aircraft seating, *see* Seating comfort, aircraft
Airfares:
intra-European, 86, 164–75
charter and inclusive tour, 168–69, 170
discount, 164–65, 169–71
examples of, 172–74
official, 165–68
travel within a country, 167
see also Air travel within Europe
transatlantic:
APEX, 7–8, 20–21, 23, 28–31, 34, 86, 91
bulk, 6, 8, 44, 53–57, 72, 92–112 *passim*

Business Class, 7, 8, 75, 166
charter, 8, 44–45, 92–112 *passim*
discount, 6, 24, 28, 57, 66–73
excursion, 11
First Class, 7, 8, 75
First Class Charter, 8, 76
full-fare Economy Class, 7, 8, 38, 85, 166
geographical variation within the United States, 8–9
group and tour status, 37
how to use this guide, 21
for last-minute travel, 59–60
on low-fare airlines, 6, 8, 38, 40, 44, 92–111 *passim*
1988 outlook for, 30–31, 38, 44–45, 54, 69, 89–112
open-jaw routes, 11, 45, 90, 121
promotional, 28, 35–37
restrictions on, 10–11, 27–28, 29, 30, 34, 37, 55, 91–111 *passim*
Round-the-World, 7, 37–38
seasonal variations in, 9–10, 54, 90